English and the OFSTED Experience

Bob Bibby and Barrie Wade

with an introductory chapter by

Trevor Dickinson

David Fulton Publishers

London

David Fulton Publishers Ltd
2 Barbon Close, London WC1N 3JX

First published in Great Britain by
David Fulton Publishers 1995

Note: The right of Bob Bibby and Barrie Wade to be identifed as the authors of this work has been asserted by them in accordance with the Copyright, Designs and Patents Act 1988.

British Library Cataloguing in Publication Data

A catalogue record for this book is available from the British Library

ISBN 1–85346–357–4

Typeset by Harrington & Co, London
Printed in Great Britain by BPC Books and Journals, Exeter

Contents

QUALITY IN SECONDARY SCHOOLS AND COLLEGES SERIES

Series Editor, Clyde Chitty

This new series publishes on a wide range of topics related to successful education for the 11–19 age group. It reflects the growing interest in whole-school curriculum planning together with the effective teaching of individual subjects and themes. There will also be books devoted to management and administration, examinations and assessment, pastoral care strategies, relationships with parents and governors and the implications for schools of changes in teacher education.

Early titles include:

Foreword

This important and unusual book provides six fascinating and revealing case-studies telling the inside story of the inspection of English under the new OFSTED régime. Six very different schools were selected, covering the age range 9 to 18, and, in each case, key personnel were invited to describe their involvement and reflect upon their experiences.

It is, of course, quite understandable that teachers should feel nervous and apprehensive about the prospect of being observed and assessed. Many look back with fond nostalgia to the days when Her Majesty's Inspectorate (HMI) was responsible for the inspection of schools in England and Wales. In the current political climate, the virtual abolition of HMI and the creation of OFSTED are easily viewed as important elements in a concerted government campaign to make teachers more accountable, more willing to become the passive deliverers of centrally-determined and centrally-controlled curricula. Yet, as the authors point out, however able and effective individual HMIs were under the old system, their practice was essentially secretive. By contrast, OFSTED's *Handbook for the Inspection of Schools* is a publicly available document, and it is at least possible for publicly declared criteria to be debated. English teachers need to be actively involved in the creation of a genuine 'interpretive community' in the teaching of their subject.

At the same time, there is a strong case for harnessing the OFSTED inspection process as a powerful weapon for change. For this to happen, it needs to be freed from government interference and allowed to become part of the drive to improve the quality of the learning experience in all our schools.

Clyde Chitty
Birmingham
February 1995

Preface

The Education (Schools) Act of 1992 heralded the end of Her Majesty's Inspectorate of schools, which for the previous 150 or so years had been responsible for the inspection of schools in England and Wales. Her Majesty's Inspectorate (HMI) was replaced by the newly created Office for Standards in Education, otherwise and immediately known as OFSTED. Commencing in 1993, OFSTED absorbed the remaining HMIs and under the direction of Professor Stewart Sutherland, who was appointed to the office of Her Majesty's Chief Inspector (HMCI), set about developing the new system of inspecting every school in England and Wales on a four-yearly basis, as laid out in the Education Act. The new system involved the training of large numbers of people, by far the majority of whom were or had been involved in educational work of one form or another, in the operation of the OFSTED *Framework for Inspection* and the setting up of a competitive tendering process, whereby registered inspectors submitted bids for schools they wished to inspect.

A quarter of the total of approximately 5500 state secondary schools – independent schools were for some mysterious reason excluded from this inspection process – was inspected during the first year of OFSTED's operation between September 1993 and July 1994. All the ten subjects of the National Curriculum, plus religious education, were inspected and reported on.

So what was it like, this new system? Because of our background and expertise, we decided to focus on the inspection of English and subject the system to some scrutiny. How did it feel to be an English teacher in one of those schools? How did it feel to be an English inspector working within the OFSTED system? And what impact did the OFSTED inspection have on those being inspected, before the inspection, during it and afterwards?

To find out the answers to these questions, we identified six very different schools which were inspected during the first year of OFSTED – an inner city 11–16 comprehensive school, a county town 11–16 denominational comprehensive school, a 9–13 new town grant-maintained middle school, a rural 11–18 comprehensive school, an urban 11–18 grant-maintained girls' grammar school and a rural 11–16 secondary modern school. In all but the last case (where the English inspector was not given permission by his LEA to participate), we interviewed four key personnel – the headteacher, the head of English, a member of the English department and the English inspector – to ascertain their views and feelings about this new system. From those interviews we have put together six case studies which tell the inner stories of the inspections of each of those schools.

The results are six fascinating yet different case studies, which form the heart of this book. In order to protect confidentiality, the names of places and people have been changed. In some cases, further minor disguise has been necessary. However, we are confident that what is written is as accurate as it could be in terms of representing the perceptions of those involved. It is our belief that the experiences of those concerned during the first year of this new system can act as pointers to those who come after them.

Our first section is given over to an account, written in his own inimitable style and from his unique perspective by former HMI Trevor Dickinson, of what it was like being an HMI involved in inspecting English. Readers will no doubt compare Trevor's account with those of the English inspectors working within the OFSTED regime, who are quoted in the accompanying case studies.

The concluding section of the book seeks to draw together the threads of the experiences described herein and to point to ways in which the inevitable stresses of an OFSTED inspection may be reduced. At the same time, it addresses the issues from the perspectives both of those being inspected and of those inspecting.

Whether you are about to undergo an OFSTED inspection or whether you have already had the experience, this book provides you with opportunities to reflect upon the experience in the company of colleagues who have been there and have the T-shirts!

We would like to thank the contributors from Bingley Community School, St Augustine's RC High School, Newton Middle School, Sheriff High School, Queen Mary's Girls' Grammar School, and Axminster Modern School, and those who inspected English in each school. Without their words, this book could not have been written.

CHAPTER 1

Inspecting into Godliness: A Personal View

Trevor Dickinson

Wondering if John Major's really read Anthony Trollope ever since I saw him miming the Warden's playing of his violin (which in reality was a cello too big, I imagine, for most chins), I take my title from Trollope, the inspectorial postman – an early version, I suppose, of Sir Ron Dearing. I forget where it's from: I suspect it's from a letter quoted by Victoria Glendinning in her marvellous biography of Trollope. But, on reading it last year, I instantly jotted the phrase down in my diary. It seemed to me to be an important reminder for all involved in devising or insisting, for whatever reason, upon inspection procedures.

You cannot inspect people into godliness.

I taught for 14 years in England and in Canada before succumbing, in 1968, to the temptations of advisory work for the Education Authority in Sheffield. Three years later I slid up the greasy pole of Her Majesty's Inspectorate, where I remained enchained, not totally unhappily, for the next 20 years.

To both advisory and inspectorial work I took, at the outset, a fair degree of suspicion and distrust. This scepticism, perhaps cynicism, had its roots in the long-standing attitudes of many practising teachers towards inspectors and advisers. We saw them, largely (as we sometimes did headteachers and teacher-trainers), I confess, as refugees from the classroom, running heavy-booted from their own pedagogical inadequacies.

My own suspicions of the process had not been much diminished by the very few classroom encounters I had had with inspectors during my teaching career.

In Kent, in about 1960, while head of an English department, I was inspected by an LEA inspector for one lesson. That lesson, again I confess with no pride, was on advertising. It was prepared hurriedly in the staff-room over coffee with the help of colleagues. I quickly forewarned the Year 7 grammar class that they were to be visited by a lady (for that is what they were in those days – especially to grammar school teachers) who wanted to see how well they could talk and conduct themselves in a discussion session. They were marvellous, my role confined to that of gentle ring-master. The inspector and I then spent 40 minutes talking English-teaching matters. She departed. I, flushed with success, proceeded to a parallel Year 7 class and set about repeating the earlier lesson. It was a disaster, on the fringes of uncontrol – certainly, in today's innovative vocabulary, less than satisfactory.

Fortunately news or noise of this later sad encounter did not reach the ears of the head, who was pleased to tell me how impressed the inspector had been with my work!

And then came Ontario, Canada. Here, I hasten to say, the ordeal of being inspected was never eagerly anticipated by most teachers, since grades were awarded by the Provincial inspectors, grades which had a substantial bearing on salary and, indeed, on contract. If memory serves me right, the highest Grade 7 was only awarded to those who had, in addition to proved classroom strengths, evidence of relevant publication.

I managed a Grade 6 – again a result of freak conditions. I had taught a Grade 13 class in the morning. I think we were looking at Book 1 of *Paradise Lost*. In the afternoon the inspector called to see me teaching a parallel Grade 13 class. At least a third of this class comprised students who, because of the school's backwood attitudes to private study, had been through the same text just a few hours earlier: the visiting inspector was greatly impressed by the keen knowledge of this class, the students' ability to engage in informed discussion, their tight grasp of text, their clear ability to cross-refer to other poetry.

I hope this long introduction is not thought to be mere space-filler. It really is an attempt to make clear my own awareness of the obstacles of resentment and suspicion which face any inspector, hard hurdles to overcome. Alongside that awareness there always rested for me, especially as an HMI, a firm and unyielding conviction that the stress of inspection in the classroom was likely to lead more teachers to under-perform rather than to rise above themselves. Of course, there were always inspection constants. The body of writing which pupils had produced was unlikely to have been much increased. The nature of writing, its range and the ways in which teachers had responded to that writing tended to be beyond tampering to gratify the inspectorial eye.

The stock cupboard's warts could hardly be hidden. Reading logs could only with the greatest of difficulty be contrived. In the unlikely event of such contrivance, talk with the readers themselves could make deception all too plain.

Despite these constants, the classroom presence of the inspector, I always had to keep reminding myself, was likely to alter the nature of the negotiations within it – between teacher and taught, between taught and taught. However sensitively an inspector sought to approach the task of inspection, the fly on the wall was visible. The notebook threatened – even if the only note made was a reminder to buy sausages on the way home.

Certainly, even at the end of a 20-year span, I remained ever unsure of how much and when to intervene in the progress of a lesson. I remain haunted by my early endeavours in a prestigious independent school to join in what I was taking to be a sixth-form discussion of excellent quality only to be politely asked by the teacher to allow him to get on and cover essential ground. At the same time I can recall meeting more than a few teachers whose confidence, they told me, was inclined to leak rapidly away when they were visited by the silent inspector in a dark and sinister corner.

On my most recent brief flirtation with inspection – in Hong Kong, armed with the OFSTED inspection schedules – I found myself still dilemma-horned. Conscious of the eternal temptation of the ageing and the elderly to yearn for past and better days, I took little joy in the oppression of a battery of questions about the quality of teaching and learning, about the evidence of knowledge gained (harder to detect sometimes than the schedule devisers seem to imagine). The sight of those schedules must have added to teachers' anxieties, however discreetly I tried to play them down, however much I tried to persuade teachers to ignore their presence. A key certainty is that they made me even more nervous than I am properly and naturally inclined to be on inspection duties.

These schedules were, of course, there in various embryonic forms towards the end of my working life as an HMI: they did little to cheer my final years in which I drew my greatest comfort from a retreat to the securer ground of responsibilities in the school library territory. There seemed to me to be about them (and about the new inspection strategies) a feel-the-width, number-crunching aspect all too clearly aligned to political dreams of published league tables. I admit that the schedule haunted me probably as much as my presence haunted the teacher. They were in the nature of a distraction from what was actually going on. Constantly I was worried that I was not getting something down on paper. It was all a far cry from the world I entered in 1971. The sight of a team of HMIs clustered daily around a conference blackboard entering up the 1–5 gradings for the lessons observed was beyond all our youthful inspectorial imaginings.

I have no illusions about that past – well very few. Despite the occasional outpourings of belatedly regretful praise from headteachers and their staffs for the qualities of HMI compared with the men and women from OFSTED, visits from HMI were, in reality, rarely welcomed unalloyed in the old days. There were exceptions to this rule, I think, when an English specialist was in some kind of regular and fairly frequent contact with English (or other) departments or schools in his or her local or divisional patch. It was then not unknown for HMI to be invited to join in with some departmental activity. It was possible on some occasions to be invited to teach. (I still remember my teaching wife asking if I had had control problems with the two small sixth-form groups I taught during a member of staff's absence at what was then Bishop Henshaw School in Rochdale! I can still remember more painfully the outcome of my accepting the head's invitation to read to a nursery class in the same Authority – very much a Grade 5 occasion!)

These one-day visits to English departments in one's 'patch' were not always easy. Too much often had to be discovered in too little time – about staffing, accommodation, equipment and resources, organisation, examination results and so much more. Then there was as wide a range of classroom and written work to see as was possible in the time left: all this was the prelude to a quick jotting down of what was to be said to the head and head of department at the end of a crammed day.

How useful this was to the schools it is hard to say. But it does have to be said that the inspection process was learned over the course of a year's probation, not in five days. It was learned at the feet of and by the sides of some pretty skilled inspectorial operators, who, in addition to their years, had also the benefit of seeing schools of all kinds in all parts of the country. They had also the benefit of excellent information networks through their engagement in in-service (INSET) work for and with teachers; through good HMI specialist committee structures; and through a steady flow of paper.

Unease about the one-day effort led to a number of modifications. There was, bold venture, the two-day visit! More daring still, there was the two-day visit by two HMIs. These brought with them the bonus of further INSET for HMI themselves. I still treasure the memory of being able to learn, after nearly 20 years in the Inspectorate, from my more recently appointed friends in the North West, Pat Brain, Frances Findlay and Mollie Sayer.

The two-day visit also lent itself to some of the survey work that I remember being involved in in Rochdale, Wigan and Sefton. Again, we hunted in pairs, allowing ourselves, therefore, a total of four days in each school. Armed with information provided by the school beforehand about accommodation, finance, resources, organisation, planning, staffing and staff development, we were thus able to concentrate our inspectorial activity on directly observing and talking with departments and those they taught. So, in Wigan, for instance, some 106 lessons were observed in a couple of days. Meetings were held with all departments. The aim of being of assistance to the LEA and its officers was met in part by the publication of a 16-page report: it was met in part by later holding a meeting for all interested English teachers in the LEA at which some of the written report's details were given more substantial illustrative flesh.

A major difference between this kind of activity and that now engaging OFSTED inspectors rests in the absence then of publicly declared criteria. Our main concern was to look at the quality of children's work in the areas of talking, listening, reading and writing. The hope was, I suppose, that the lengthy training of HMI and the conference and paper networking referred to above would lead to valid judgements likely to be made equally by whatever inspector happened to visit a particular class. It was, despite a fair degree of common view among HMI English specialists, perhaps a fairly pious hope. That said, I cannot escape the view that all the current paraphernalia of criteria does not dispose of the chance that two OFSTED English inspectors might, for a whole range of reasons, political, historical or social, for instance, see particular worlds very, very differently. Objective judgement is a myth.

Of course, the smarter readers were able to look at HMI reports, once Sir Keith Joseph had insisted on their being published, and backtrack their way through to some of the criteria that underpinned HMI's judgements. In exactly the same way alert librarians were able to refute the charge that HMI had no library yardsticks. The backtrackers' task was eased to some extent by the publication in the Wigan and Sefton Survey Reports of Appendix accounts of good lessons observed. So, for instance, a Year 8 lesson is described in the following not untypical terms:

> A top set class settles quickly, listens carefully to instructions and sets eagerly to work in groups preparing booklets, news sheets, posters, advertisements, drama scripts, reviews, puzzles, character studies relating to books they have read. Pupils talk very well about their work and make clear how it has increased their appetite for the books themselves. A table of boys talks convincingly of the way this work has increased their ability to co-operate. Pupils want to carry on during break. This is a very productive example of the

joint development of listening, talking, reading and writing. The pupils' written work is of impressive quality with firm attention to its presentation and lay-out.

Now I know, beyond doubt, that this report on Wigan work inspected in 1984 was read carefully by Sefton teachers before the small team of HMIs, operating in pairs, began its parallel onslaught upon that LEA. What HMI saw as desirable practice was there for all to see whether they were teachers, teacher-trainers, LEA advisers/inspectors or parents. There was clear, inescapable attention given in the Survey Report's lesson notes to such issues as: the importance of good quality reading by teachers; skilled reading by pupils; careful planning; match of task to ability; the need for extended talk opportunities; range of writing tasks; neat, legible presentation; dedication to task; careful and productive listening; high demand.

The main body of the Wigan English Survey Report drew attention in different ways to what were described as representation 'in microcosm of some long-standing national and widespread deficiencies in English teaching'.

It spoke of the need to exploit better some younger pupils' natural linguistic strengths; the need for more pupils to be given the chance to frame their own classroom questions; the need to develop more enthusiasm for reading and especially for poetry; the need to make more accessible a wider range of less tatty books. The Report gave hints about some less successful approaches towards reading aloud. It drew attention to the misuse of textbooks and the widespread application of the same exercise to all members of classes irrespective of clearly diagnosed need. It bewailed the fact that, in some cases, such exercisery far out-weighed pupils' opportunities for continuous writing for a wider range of audiences. It laid substantial weight upon the need for departments to develop meaningful, effective policies for the marking of pupils' written work – and much more. So, again, coming in from the rear end of the inspection telescope, teachers and other readers can have been left in little doubt as to what HMI hoped to see.

There was no grand panoply of inspection criteria for this work. There was no obsession with form-filling. There was, in my view, less danger of inspection wood of real worth being obscured by paper trees.

That was a lesson firmly embedded in the great HMI National Secondary Survey now sadly shrouded in the fading mists of time. The HMI English specialist's broad task at that time was to visit schools on week-long inspections to investigate the issue of Language across the Curriculum, a concept seemingly just being re-discovered, if somewhat shallowly, by the politicians. There was no lengthy *aide-mémoire*. The main requirements were a careful ear and a speedy pen. The task was to take heed of language and learning events without the danger, as I see it, of obsession with tunnel-visioned completion of an OFSTED-style worksheet. The jewels of classroom observation were endlessly mined. The price paid was in the grim task of retrieving and re-expressing it all in report form. And that, I suppose, is why there followed the less risky retreat into box-filling and calculation.

I am not consumed with nostalgia for those old inspection days. My recent experience of being plucked from my reading chair does not make me eager to return to the inspectorial fray. Indeed, I turned down last year an invitation to inspect English in Derby. (I've been to Derby!) In the last month, I've turned down two invitations to inspect Initial Teacher Training, puzzled by the need to drag me from my book when so many of my erstwhile colleagues have been lured or driven into premature retirement. The fact that I was assured that the work was very lucrative neither excited nor cheered me.

Even had things stayed the way they were before the early squirmings of the blind, newly born gerbil fathered by Kenneth Baker with the then Mrs Thatcher as its surrogate mother, I think I would have been more than reluctant to continue in the inspectorial role.

Quite frankly, although I enjoyed the privilege of visiting and inspecting schools of all kinds over the entire length and breadth of England – plus a brief excursion to Munster – I always found inspection daunting. I was always conscious of the threat I posed to teachers however hard I tried, genuinely, to persuade them before and during the inspection that I was more terrified than they. I was always afraid that the snapshots I took of a department's work – over a day or two or over a week – might be taken with a faulty film or a cheap camera or in poor lighting conditions.

I suppose too that, as an inspector, I was always beset by memories of my own inadequacies as a teacher, the many sins of omission and commission of which I still, 26 years after I finished teaching, regularly dream in a sweat of terror. (The most frequently recurring dream is of teaching an O level class on the Monday before the English literature exam on the Wednesday. Some bright spark reminds that we haven't yet studied the key set text, *Macbeth*. 'Don't worry,' I say. 'We can tackle that tomorrow!') My genuine and convinced attempts to persuade others that it is perfectly possible to be a less than adequate teacher but a good inspector (or teacher-trainer) ring hollowly in my own ears.

As an HMI too I was uncomfortably aware of the fact that teachers' own personal pastoral needs can, on occasion, be no less significant than those of their charges. So how was I, unhappily married and going through divorce proceedings at one chunk of my HMI life, to inspect sensitively teachers whose own personal lives might be in some disarray? (I found it hard, as I still do, to escape the memory of the school I inspected for a week quite early in my HMI days, the headteacher of which was in the throes of a personal tragedy which resulted, not long after the inspection, in the suicide of his daughter-in-law and her murder of his grandchildren. Under-performance in such a setting might be forgiven.)

The need to inspect sensitively was one of the early lessons I had imperfectly to learn. I had to learn also, in those early days, to follow the advice of an excellent mentor of the old school – to try to judge a school or a department by what it declared it was trying to do, and not by some fanciful blue-print of my own.

I also learned to recognise the value of the suggestion that the inspection process ought to focus powerfully on whatever strengths could be located. It ought to leave those inspected able to carry on their work in a positive frame of mind although left in no doubt about what might need to be remedied. They ought, that is, to feel and perform better for having been inspected.

It is hard to say whether or not that ever was the reality. It is more difficult to gauge from the distance of pushing three years' retirement whether or not it is the case today. Certainly the occasional newspaper accounts of inspection findings suggest a harsher, sometimes more ruthless kind of inspection world. If that is the sad scenario, it may be a consequence of the present government's obsession with league-tabling. It may be a result of the painful winnowing of HMI, the remnants of a once-proud and determinedly professional body oddly translated, in its search for longer life, into that Soviet-style Thought Police which Dr Sheila Lawlor, Director of the Centre for Policy Studies, accused it of being in its pre-OFSTED/DFE days. Muscles may be being flexed by a yuppier crew.

It occurs to me also to ponder the possibilities that rest beneath the fact that the independent OFSTED teams have, I gather, been assessed by HMI at the same time as managing the inspection process. Inspection is hard enough anyway without the shadow of some ambitious latter-day Matthew Arnold lurking conspicuously in the background and revealing nothing of his or her assessment mind. This, along with the current government's creation, through its various charters, of a gripe society, may lead to the temptation to accentuate the negative in schools' practice.

In some respects, this may not be a bad thing. I recall once being told by Rochdale's chief adviser, when I was HMI district inspector for that

LEA, that I wandered the local schools distributing praise like some educational Santa Claus. I was hurt by that. I was sure that his vision was born of the failure of headteachers to pass on to the LEA's advisory service anything other than the praise I had benevolently bestowed. On the other hand, I confess that there was a speck of truth in the charge.

In my anxiety to be loved, I suspect I may have sometimes ducked out of telling some of the more painful truths – as I had seen them. I think also that from time to time I must have judged that no progress was likely in the areas on which I might have put in the inspectorial boot. From time to time, even now, I recognise that in my desire to build up and sustain some teachers' confidence, I put at risk my greater and more essential obligation – that of seeing that the children were getting the best educational deal, that they were in no way being sold short.

That said, however, I remind myself that I was part of a system in which the masking of some painful educational realities was par for the course – if it meant masking some of those realities from the eyes and thought processes of the politicians. For those realities were sometimes obscured by the process of HMI report vetting. The report (for instance one's 800 word Full Inspection paragraph on the work in English or the whole report on the work of half-a-dozen English departments or an account of the provision and use of 42 primary school libraries) would go through a rigorous fine tooth-combing first by one's peers, then by one's staff inspector and divisional inspector. At a later stage, if things were thought to be risky or, I remember once in my own case, when my deep anger at the library short-changing children ran away with me in wild and whirling words, then chief inspectors would want their say, and, of course, civil servants would seek further to ensure that nothing slipped by which would embarrass the government unduly or seek to suggest that extra funding might be a solution.

This clearly led to some huge and pretty unacceptable delays between inspection and publication. It also resulted all too often in a prose style widely regarded as the Rolls Royce of blandness. None the less, the report writing process and the involvement of all inspection team members in the scrutiny process did have the advantage of broadening awareness. It was a means of furthering a shared understanding of those unstated criteria referred to earlier. One key, if less admirable, advantage in this marathon was the remoteness of any possible litigation arising from inspection – a prospect less remote for current can-carriers, it is rumoured, under the new inspection arrangements!

Well, I continue to be grateful to my parents for timing my conception so immaculately. I am relieved beyond measure that I am not part of the current processes of inspection. I stay amazed at friends and colleagues who whinged for years to the point of ill-health about the rigours of old-style inspection, the lonely hours in hotel rooms, the seemingly endless panel meetings in which we argued the school's proper toss – who, desperate for cash or freedom from oblivion, post-retirement have embarked upon the new privatised inspection ship. They moan no less loudly: they still feel the chest pains and suspect the ulcers. But they seem to me to lack the benefits of the professional networkery that I so highly valued.

With no desire then to return to the old inspectorial fray and certainly no desire to cash in upon the new one (despite the fact that my dormer roof is in need of expensive cowboy replacement), I do not look back with total gloom upon my HMI life. Sharing with teachers the terrors of the first day of any inspection, I recall happily the many occasions on which inspectors were told by teachers that things had got steadily better during the course of the week. I still recall the happy relief of many a department when the final hour of debriefing had gone well, despite our mutual terrors. I can still recall the head of department who said, after I had reported on the week, that I had given his team something to live up to.

More painfully, I can recall with no pride and much shame the tears of the Rotherham English teacher to whom I reported back about the library for which she was responsible. What was it I said? How had I said it? Did my scurrying to the head and to her line-manager deputy head to remind them that the library's shortcomings were all in their wormy can have a soothing impact? I suspect not. (For all its attention to ensuring that reports were couched in the least reprehensible of terms, the Inspectorate did little to monitor or improve our spoken feed-back skills.)

Despite all the dangers of sentimentality which have marked my entire life, I have to say that the abiding memories of my inspection life are those generated by the real blessing of schools, the children they are meant to serve. I remember frequently, in the way of age, the six year old in Rochdale who told me I should trim my eyebrows: I looked like Dracula. I recall Tracey from Sir John Cass School in Stepney bound for Sussex University, paying moving tribute to the head of English who had been like a father to her. I recall with some small smug pride the 15-year-old girl who astonished the teacher who had taught her all year when she talked to me with sustained and articulate clarity about her attitudes to English. With angry pain, I remember the ten year old in Rochdale who told me she would be unemployed when she grew up. 'It's obvious isn't it?' I remember, an odd feature of inspection duties, visiting Lancashire for the privilege of hearing youngsters deciding at great and energetic length on their Children's Book of the Year. I remember seeing children at a Leeds special school preparing for the visit of a spaceman (that is, a member of the Leeds Theatre in Education team in motor-cycle gear), one small boy sitting on my knee to rehearse his offering to the spaceman of *Tie a Yellow Ribbon Round the Old Oak Tree*. I remember the cheering sight of a Downs Syndrome girl in a tiny rural Barnsley school reading and writing with supreme confidence. And so much more.

If those experiences are lost to the new breed of inspectors, then it's a shabbier world than it ought to be. I can't believe that they are. Those fine experiences and encounters certainly will continue to exist in worlds where inspectors share the notion expressed in Rosellen Brown's novel, *Before and After*, that there ought to be an eleventh commandment: Honour thy children! That eleventh commandment needs to rest alongside a sentence from a novel by Leon Garfield. I think it is *The Sound of Coaches* – or is it *The Strange Affair of Adelaide Harris?* Anyway, the sentence that has stayed with me for many a long year is: Many a man is made good by being thought so. I can't promise that all my work as HMI was as informed by that thought as it should have been. But I did keep reminding myself of the importance of those words, especially in these more recent years, when teachers seem to have excited especial press and political contempt. No less now than in the midst of my HMI life, those charged with or choosing the task of inspecting schools need to keep firmly in their minds the fact that teaching is no soft option. It is a risky task undertaken more than ever under the public gaze.

Those who inspect them must recognise the reality that today's teachers teach in troubled, testing and league-tabled times. Their work is exposed to ignorance and to dangerous myth and malice. They undertake a task more difficult than that ever envisaged by those who taught them or, for the most part, by those who inspect them. Clearly their teacherly interests should not, must not be put before those of the children they teach. None the less, they do deserve inspectors' genuinely respectful attention and sensitive sympathy. They do deserve accurate awareness of the social circumstances in which they work. They do need careful inspection by inspectors who realise their own professional frailty, inspectors who realise that inspection into godliness is a non-starter.

CHAPTER 2

Like Preparing for the Cup Final: Bingley Community School (11–16)

Background

Bingley Community School is situated in the heart of one of central England's largest cities and its pupil population fully reflects the multi-ethnic community on which it draws. The school serves an urban area where many families live in poverty, where housing is often inadequate, and where infant mortality rates, together with levels of childhood accident and illness, are very high. Almost half of the pupils at the school come from homes where there is no-one in employment and, for those who are employed, work is too frequently part-time, low-paid and temporary. Almost a third of pupils live with only one parent, and many have unsettled home and family backgrounds. The cycle of deprivation is reflected in low self-esteem, and in problems of language and communication which prevail among adults as well as children, regardless of ethnic background.

The above comments, taken in slightly amended form from the OFSTED report on the school, give some indication of the sort of school to which Bill Wright was appointed headteacher some seven years prior to the OFSTED inspection. He himself had only one previous experience of an inspection and that was very early in his career when the school he was then teaching in received an HMI inspection, which in general he found to be 'a reasonable experience'. He remembers particularly an incident where the HMI inspecting his subject borrowed a set of books belonging to one of his lower sets in the fourth year and mislaid them on a bus!

Through a mixture of personal politicking with local industry and with the community, of successful bidding for major projects funded by city and central government money, and, as he will admit, of good fortune in the school being situated in an area designated for urban regeneration, Bill Wright has managed to improve the building stock and the resources of the school, which once housed 1500 pupils but now has only 520. In recent years there has been a trend back to the school and numbers have increased steadily, as the capital investment in the school and its increased success in serving its immediate community have become apparent.

The school takes pupils aged 11 to 16 years, almost half of whom have reading-age scores below nine years of age on entry to the school, based on results of nationally standardised tests administered by the school. Almost 6 per cent of pupils have statements of special educational need, many of these being educated for part of their time in the special unit for pupils with moderate learning difficulties which is housed within the Bingley school buildings. Three members of staff are funded under Section 11 of the Local Government Act (1966) to provide support for pupils whose first language is not English. Overall GCSE results are well below both city and national standards.

At the time of the inspection, Doug Collins, who had worked in the school for over 20 years and was now a head of faculty, was acting head of English pending a new appointment after the recent move of the previous departmental head to a new school. Paul Lawrence, by contrast, who had trained for teaching at the city's university, was only in his second year of teaching.

Dramatis personae

Bill Wright – headteacher (29 years teaching experience, including seven as headteacher).

Doug Collins – acting head of English (26 years teaching experience, 21 of them at Bingley Community School).

Paul Lawrence – English teacher (two years teaching experience).

Colin Forster – English inspector (14 years teaching experience, seven years as LEA advisory teacher for English, one term as LEA English inspector).

Before the inspection

The announcement by the government of the new system of OFSTED school inspections created by the Education (Schools) Act of 1992 was greeted negatively at Bingley School. Doug Collins saw it as 'part and parcel of the anti-teacher approach which had crept into the DFE' with 'teachers being treated like naughty pupils by "our" teachers'. He linked it with other examples of what he termed 'retrogressive legislation' such as the compulsory examinations for 16 year olds, the SATs, and particularly the loss of 100 per cent coursework assessment in English where he had seen 'children gaining enormously from this approach when the teacher has control over what books and what approaches to use'. Doug thought it was a throwback to times of judgemental inspection and, as he said on hearing of it initially, 'I was agin it'.

Paul Lawrence, on the other hand, who had himself been at school through some of the period when the government was legislating for change in the educational system, was more concerned about 'the people who would be involved in OFSTED' and whether 'they'd be looking for things in English teaching which were against my ideals'.

Headteacher Bill Wright was rather cynical at first, because he was enthusiastic about the city's quality development initiative, which was much more of a collaborative venture between local advisers and the schools. He felt that the adviser system in the city was good 'with advisers coming into classrooms and helping' and this had 'broken down a lot of fear and suspicion'. He also felt that appraisal had 'helped to generate a whole feeling of collaboration in the assessment of each other, bridging the gap between where you are and where you want to be, and supporting career development'. So the new model of inspection did not sit easily with this. However, because of the changes in classroom practice which he felt had been a feature of his seven years as headteacher, he thought that 'it would do us some good to be inspected' and 'I could see advantages to be gained'. He told the staff that he expected them to be among the first schools to be inspected and that he thought it was 'appropriate that people came and really assessed how we were getting on'.

On hearing that Bingley School was to be inspected in the first term of the new system, perceptions were slightly different. Doug Collins remembers:

> There was a lot of talk that they'd got it in for the city and that they were picking on schools in the city where they thought the city might be lacking. I didn't particularly agree with any of that.

Paul Lawrence felt that people calmed down a lot when they heard that the dates of the inspection were fixed:

The beginning of term would have messed up the summer. The time it was was a perfect opportunity to get into the stride of the new year.

Bill Wright thought it was 'a good time to be inspected' although he was sorry that he had to 'read about it in the local press before the letter came – but I'm used to that!' He also felt the autumn term was a good time:

I don't quite know why, except it's fairly early on in the school year when you're supposed to have your act together. You've got your development plan and it's in its fairly early stages. It's a more promising time to be inspected.

The contract for the OFSTED inspection of the school was not won by the city's inspectorate but by that of a neighbouring Local Education Authority. When the school heard of this in the July preceding the inspection, reaction was again mixed.

'Didn't bother me! They could have come from the Isle of Skye', was Doug Collins's reaction, while Paul Lawrence recalls that, 'Lots of rumours abounded about the team, some of which hit the mark though some didn't. Some rumours were just scaremongering – stories that had been mixed up.' Bill Wright claimed that he hadn't wanted the city inspectorate team to win the contract, although 'because of my political perspective – I didn't believe in the privatisation of it all', he was glad that it was an LEA inspection team.

Once the membership of the inspection team was known, Bill Wright 'hawked the team list round a bit with headteacher colleagues and got a little bit of feedback' and at his first meeting with the registered inspector he raised his concerns about one member of the team who was known to some staff from previous involvement with the school in examination work. Doug Collins had no prior knowledge of anyone from the team, least of all of the English inspector, while Paul Lawrence was 'reassured by hearing from an English advisory teacher in the city and from one of my tutors at the university that Colin Forster was alright'. His reassurance came from the knowledge that, 'People who shared similar ideas on English teaching' thought thus. This made him feel more confident about what was going to happen.

External preparation for the inspection was offered by the city inspectorate and four inspectors spent a week in the school, homing in on certain aspects of the OFSTED *Framework for Inspection*. 'Staff reaction was mixed', recalls Bill Wright, although he thought it was of some value because 'certain aspects of management that you don't get round to doing' they picked up but 'it didn't tell us anything we didn't already know and there was some nit-picking which was irritating'. Doug Collins felt that 'after the pre-inspection – "the dress rehearsal" – I was glad that they hadn't won the contract'. He himself had no classroom observation, which seemed to focus disproportionately on the then head of English and it was 'of no value whatsoever personally or to the department. We didn't do anything as a result of it that we wouldn't have been doing anyway. Nobody gained anything from it, unless it was to demystify the whole process.' Paul Lawrence has no recall of who visited the school or for how long. He attended a conference at the university where a former HMI for English explained the new system and this he found helpful.

The main substance of the internal preparations made by the English department for the inspection was in putting together the departmental handbook. This was handicapped by the fact that the then head of department left at the end of the summer term, leaving effectively only two specialist English teachers, who 'had confidence in each other' and 'discussed schemes of work together', though both admitted that there was little of substance written down. Paul recalls 'spending numerous hours at the computer contributing to the handbook'. Much of it was already in existence but some was new and 'some of it was good, but some was just decoration'. Doug remembers 'a bit of panic' on seeing other departmental handbooks being run off in the reprographics room and being told, 'This is volume two!' He also recalls someone who had been on an OFSTED training course and who came back to the school to say, 'Don't build paper castles as a protection against OFSTED'. He feels that 'management here, perhaps unintentionally, made the handbooks take on greater significance than was necessary'. He went further:

> It's got to the stage – and it's one of the reasons why I'm planning to take early retirement in a year's time – like in the army where, if it doesn't move, paint it; in teaching, if you do it, record it. That is a blind alley. It's not the direction English teaching went when it was at its most fruitful.

Bill Wright, though taking the view that 'you shouldn't throw the whole schedule of the school out of gear', nevertheless felt that 'it's a bit of a set piece, like preparing for the cup final, and you have to take it seriously'. Consequently, he felt that the efforts made by the school in preparation for the inspection were worthwhile.

At this point, Colin Forster, who had recently been appointed to his post as English inspector in the LEA which had won the contract to inspect Bingley Community School, was still awaiting his training as an OFSTED inspector. This training occurred during the first week of the school summer holidays and Colin recalls feeling 'shattered because of the timing – the end of a hectic term' and 'stressed because of the perceived hidden agenda – would we be good OFSTED inspectors? i.e.

would we meet the government's agenda?' He also had no prior experience of inspecting, although he had extensive experience in the field of English teaching as a successful head of English and subsequently as an advisory teacher for English, involved in the National Writing Project and the Language in the National Curriculum (LINC) Project. All through the week of training he felt that he was 'being watched all the time'. He himself had experienced an HMI inspection very early in his career, about which he 'was not bothered because the HMIs who conducted it were very open and approachable', and later had a full LEA inspection of the school in which he was head of English, from which he recalls the 'pompous manner of the chief inspector strutting around the staffroom', although the English inspector was sympathetic and helpful.

Colin's view of the stated OFSTED intention of 'improvement through inspection' is that this is a secondary issue – a sort of 'development through the back door'. He believes that it is possible to 'network good ideas and good practice' through inspection and that the preparation for inspection does make people 'look at areas which are weak' and bring about greater sharing within departments.

Early in the autumn term Colin Forster heard that he had satisfactorily completed his OFSTED training. His first view of Bingley Community School came from the pre-inspection documentation sent to him by the registered inspector some weeks before the inspection. From this he noted that examination results were very low and that the pupils had low reading ages on entry, that there was a mixed intake from a large number of primary schools, and that this included a high ethnic minority. 'Obviously the department was in a state of change with a temporary head of English' and the departmental handbook left him with 'no clear perception of the mapping of the English curriculum'. He knew nothing otherwise about the school or its staff.

So there they were a few days before the actual event. Bill Wright found himself checking the first-aid boxes and the strip lights and making sure there was no litter. Although he was feeling 'quite relaxed about policies that were still in the process of formulation', he was worried about the weather because snow was forecast, weather in which 'the school doesn't show itself at its best', and also because there was a lot of influenza around and he was 'really anxious about staff absence'. He also revealingly commented that, 'I realised that OFSTED was an assessment of my own leadership which had produced big changes in the school.'

Doug Collins's attitude was quite clear:

> I do the best I possibly can with the kids I am given and the time I'm given. I know I'm not perfect and I'm prepared to take criticism. I do not want to pull

the wool over people's eyes. I want them to see the warts. We have tried strenuously to avoid bullshit in the handbook.

Paul Lawrence's main fear was that 'the kids wouldn't cope with the situation'. Colin Forster was unsure of 'what to expect in classrooms'.

During the inspection

Paul Lawrence recalls vividly the journey to school on the Monday of the inspection week:

> I knew I was going to be watched second lesson with my Year 10 group, because I had a kid who was being trailed. And I do remember feeling quite numb as I walked in. We sat in the staff room because we had a briefing beforehand. And as the team was introduced I could feel my stomach churning. I had a lesson beforehand which I don't know how I taught but then the lesson came and it went alright.

Bill Wright arrived at school very early, anxious because there actually was snow on the ground. 'I very quickly did my tour of the school and got my caretaker mobilised and found that everything was OK as far as the site was concerned', he recalls. Another early arrival was the recently appointed head of physical education who reassured Bill that the PE programme could go ahead as normal. By the time that the inspectors arrived and were ready to be introduced at staff briefing, he knew that there was no staff absence and felt 'reasonably OK'.

Doug Collins cannot remember arriving at school, although he did have an inspector in his first lesson, attached to a pupil in his tutor group. The inspector 'just observed what was done in tutorial time'.

Colin Forster's main concern that morning was 'finding the school and being on time'. He remembers the staff looking very apprehensive during the introductions in the staff briefing session.

By the middle of the first morning, Bill Wright felt powerless as the inspection was going on around him. He had made the decision to make himself available by being around the school and early conversations with his heads of department were reassuring. By the end of the day his feeling was 'one of relief – there were no distress signals'.

Colin Forster had a pre-arranged meeting with Doug Collins on the first morning, which Doug cannot remember, though Colin remembers that, 'It was unusual because issues concerned with the direction of the school were raised', as well as matters relating to the English department. Paul Lawrence also met Colin during the first day and found him to be 'extremely friendly, not aggressive in any way, put me at ease'.

Informal conversation in the inspectors' base during the first day 'tends to be more negative', Colin Forster observed. He found himself 'putting positive aspects forward to counteract the negatives' of fellow inspectors, was reassured to find that 'other respected colleagues were saying the same things' and was interested to notice some of his positive statements 'being echoed by other inspectors at the first team meeting'.

Colin felt there were no problems during his lesson observations and found it 'a very pleasant experience, although I was uncomfortable because I couldn't join in'. He didn't sense any undue stress among the English staff. This was echoed by both Paul and Doug. Paul remembers:

> The inspector talked before, during and after the lessons but there was no interference with the lesson. Once I'd set the task and got the kids into groups, there was interaction all the time.

Doug described a lesson with a Year 10 group:

> We had a Theatre in Education group in – purely by accident. It didn't run perfectly, there were some logistical problems. They decided the kids should break into groups of five. Can you imagine 80 kids working on a piece of improvisation in groups in a drama studio the size of a classroom? So we hastily had to hive groups off into spare rooms. But the inspector was perfectly understanding about that.

Colin Forster felt that the lessons he observed were 'representative of the normal work of the department' because much of the work clearly followed on from previous work. Doug Collins confirmed this normality because 'you couldn't do anything else in this school – our kids are too candid'. Paul Lawrence felt that staff 'generally tried to show themselves at their best' and he 'personally did lessons as I would have done – I don't play safe normally'. However, he also noted:

> You can't relax in that situation, however well the inspectors treat you. I don't think there's anything you can do. You can alleviate the stress but you can't get rid of it.

He admitted that it was perhaps easier for him since he had been observed teaching during his PGCE course at university and during his probationary year 12 months previously.

Colin found the pupils 'extremely friendly, talking openly about their work, more so than in other schools'. Paul thought the children were generally better behaved and were 'very loyal to the teachers and the school'. He cited the instance of one boy:

> Nice lad, but he hadn't been behaving particularly well in the week before the inspection. When it actually came to the inspection he was perfect in every way. The joke about it afterwards was that we said to him, 'You've set

yourself a standard now, keep up to it.' And he has done. So, for him, I think the inspection was a good thing!

Doug remembers that there was no staff absence during the inspection week, although there was one teacher who 'should have been away but she soldiered on' and that 'those of us who smoke were more than usually glad to get to the smoke room at break and lunchtime'. He also noted that the inspection team was itself being monitored by HMI during the week. 'It's like fleas on fleas', he mused.

As the week drew to a close, the English team readied themselves for hearing the findings of the inspection of their department. Doug had 'no fears whatsoever', though he confessed to 'curiosity certainly'. Paul was 'confident that things would be OK', though he was also 'prepared for disappointment at the end of it'. He was 'generally happy with the way it had gone'.

In preparing to give his oral report to Doug, Colin Forster was aware that much of what he would be saying was for the attention of the yet-to-be-appointed head of English. Nevertheless, he felt that 'the criticisms flowed from the positive comments' and that, in a way, 'it was easy to be critical about the lack of monitoring of the English curriculum because Doug was new in post'. He felt that he was able to 'identify many good features in the department' and to show 'areas for development'.

During the feedback session, Colin sensed that Doug was 'distancing himself from the report' despite invitations to join in. Doug recalls that, 'The things that were raised were things I agreed with' and that the feedback was 'good' with 'opportunities to ask questions'.

Paul Lawrence, not able to attend this session, received a summary report from Doug. 'I wished I'd been there to ask questions myself', he said. Some of the things pointed out were 'things we were aiming to do anyway, like the portfolio of pupils' work'. Also he commented:

Colin Forster thought the kids' secretarial skills were weak. I thought that was an over-generalisation but that's his professional judgement and I respect that. But overall I was reasonably happy, it was generally fair. When you think about the disasters that could have happened if you get an inspector who doesn't like your way of teaching, things not going well in the classroom, all that seems quite trivial by the time you get the actual feedback.

After the inspection

On the Friday afternoon, after the inspection team had departed, Doug Collins felt 'tired – more so than normal', Paul Lawrence was 'quite numb – a real sense of "Thank God that's over!"'. Headteacher Bill Wright had a three-hour debriefing on the whole-school issues on the Friday morning during which he felt 'OK, though there were some things I was not happy about, particularly the use of "satisfactory"'. At the end of the day, however, he felt 'deflated because it had finished, because you are running on adrenalin', although over the weekend as he thought about it he realised that positive achievements in areas such as racial harmony and improving standards had been recognised.

So the school returned to normality. The next impact of the inspection was five weeks later when the report was published. The summary paragraphs on English in the report, written by Colin Forster, included positive comments about standards in speaking and listening, about drafting of written work, about the reading support programme for weaker readers, about the quality of relationships between teachers and pupils, and about teaching that is 'supportive and encouraging'. However, attention is drawn to the inappropriateness of much of the fiction stock in the school library, to the need for improved standards in spelling and punctuation in pupils' writing, and to the inadequate monitoring of schemes of work.

Both Doug and Paul admitted that they went first of all to the report on English because 'you want to see what they've said about you'. None of it was a surprise, though both felt concerned about the reference to the library in the English section, because, as Doug pointed out, 'The library is a whole-school issue and no-one in the English department is paid for responsibility in the library.' Colin, however, felt that his comments, which referred to the fiction stock of the library, were justified because 'who else should influence the choice of fiction in the library?'

Bill Wright thought 'the overall report was very good', but 'what I wasn't so happy about was the summary report where I thought the subject comments were too brief'. Paul Lawrence thought that 'some of the points about the whole school could have been expressed better'. He confessed to being 'unsure about the meaning of some of it'. Doug Collins was more forthright:

> Let's face it, OFSTED-speak is an offence, an insult to the language. It's a green light for misunderstanding. I would have much preferred a crystal clear report, even where it said the English department must do certain things. But when it's couched in such vague generalities! If that's what English is about – the kind of language used in that report, I give up!

In response to the issues identified in the English report and in the oral feedback, the department has subsequently been working towards the collation of portfolios of assessed pupils' work, better monitoring of schemes of work and seeking to rectify the imbalance in the literary texts being used to include more with a multicultural flavour. However, as Paul Lawrence pointed out, 'There are lots of things delaying the department – lack of time, the appointment of a new head of English, the impact of Dearing.'

In order to involve all staff in the creation of the required Action Plan to address the key issues identified in the overall report, a training day was allocated by senior management and staff were divided into groups to discuss one separate issue each. Paul Lawrence admitted that 'I haven't actually seen the entire OFSTED Action Plan' and felt that 'the day might have been more beneficial if time had been spent looking at key issues in relation to schemes of work in the English department'. Doug Collins, who is also a teacher governor, was 'heavily involved in drawing up the Action Plan' although he had some difficulty in interpreting the key issues. He was convinced that 'one point is still misinterpreted by senior management' and was concerned that, in putting together the Action Plan, the school 'has to be crystal clear, whereas the inspectors can get away with woolliness'.

Final perceptions

Paul Lawrence – English teacher
Overall, the place doesn't seem to have changed. The things that needed changing according to the OFSTED report, I can't think of any evidence that they have been done. It affirmed the direction of the department – we feel vindicated as a department. Whether we're right to think that, I'm not sure. There was a positive sense of vindication. The handbook has made everyone up-to-date but it needs further development. If there hadn't been the inspection, it might not have happened. I found it deeply frustrating that I couldn't discuss lessons with the inspector. I can't see why professionals can't sit down and talk about lessons and open the gateway to professional development. To have someone of Colin Forster's experience come in and not be able to comment to me on what he saw is just loopy.

Doug Collins – head of English
It gets you to look at yourself and to articulate why you're doing what you do. You get a clearer picture of your own values, your own expectations of pupils, your own approaches to the subject. It puts you in the position where you have, like a lawyer, to prepare your case, to stand by what you believe in. I'm glad the inspection was when it was, in the light of Dearing and the subsequent changes to English, because Dearing is tightening the straps on the straitjacket already on us. But

the same result could have been achieved in different ways; for example, appraisal would have had the same result and probably other more beneficial results. It didn't need that sledgehammer to crack that particular nut.

Colin Forster – English inspector
I've had no contact subsequently with the school whatsoever. That is a huge weakness of the system. Because I would also have guessed that they would have liked as a department to discuss things with me in greater detail. I'm still slightly dubious about the value of the English inspection. Because of the strange staffing situation, I wasn't talking to the most appropriate person. If it had been a school in my own LEA, I would have made a point of going to see the new head of English when they were appointed to discuss the report with them, but of course I couldn't do that. I would hope that by the end of the inspection, as a team, we had given some recognition to what the school had achieved. For example, there had been a lot of racial tensions in the area at one time and the school had produced an environment where that was not a factor and that is a great achievement. But in the culture of league tables that is not a thing that a school gets recognition for.

Bill Wright – headteacher
It was very valuable because it actually reinforced our educational philosophy because there's always an issue about the National Curriculum, there's a tendency for some teachers to use the National Curriculum as an excuse to say that things like our mixed-ability approach, our flexible-learning approach, can't really be done any more and we need to become more formal and streamed. If you don't watch it, there's a little bit of questioning of core values. What the inspection did for me was reinforce what we were doing, that the approach was right. In fact the areas that got criticism were where there was didactic teaching. And we were ready for some rigorous analysis. And I'd pay tribute to the inspection team – they were great. They got on well with the children, they ate with the children. They actually said on the last day they felt part of the school. In fact on the last day as they were taking their boxes out to their cars, one of our louder girls called out 'See you on Monday' to the registered inspector, which was hilarious but also somehow significant.

CHAPTER 3

Pressing on the Accelerator: St Augustine's RC High School (11–16)

Background

St Augustine's RC High School is situated in a west country county town and serves a wide catchment area, which includes the county town itself, neighbouring smaller towns and the rural parts of the southern half of the county, comprising 11 Catholic parishes and eight feeder Catholic primary schools. However, 40 per cent of its pupils are non-Catholic and come from a range of other nearby primary schools. A small proportion of the intake are of ethnic minority origin, mainly Pakistani. An even smaller number of pupils – ten at the time of the inspection – are in receipt of statements of special educational need. Only 8 per cent of pupils are eligible for free school meals, from which it can be gathered that the parental population served is largely from a secure socio-economic base which is also supportive of schooling.

The school takes pupils aged 11 to 16 years and has 850 pupils on roll, fairly evenly split between each year group. GCSE examination results for each of the two years preceding the OFSTED inspection were above both local and national averages in overall terms. The school should be seen, therefore, as one where standards of achievement academically are above average, although the inspectors found 'some boys and some low achievers in Key Stage 4 who seem to be adversely affected by the banding and setting arrangements'.

St Augustine's mission statement gives prominence to the concept of faith development and to the importance of prayer and liturgical worship in the life of the school. Complementary to the OFSTED inspection, the school was inspected during the week before by a team of inspectors from the Archdiocese who reported on the school's provision for religious education and for the spiritual, moral, social and cultural development of its pupils. This team found the school to be 'a compassionate community, conscious of and committed to its Catholic foundations' and one which 'appears to be progressing in a healthy manner to new levels of achievement'.

Mavis Bentley had been at the school as deputy headteacher responsible for the curriculum for 11 years. Her only experience of school inspections previously had been one year prior to the OFSTED inspection when the LEA inspectorate had conducted a full inspection of the school. This, she recalled, 'was a very positive experience' because the school had wanted to use the inspection to help them move forward and it had 'validated their intentions'.

Helen Roberts, the head of English, who had been at St Augustine's for four years after 16 years teaching elsewhere, had also had prior experience of being inspected, in her case by an HMI team in the school she had worked in previously. She confessed to 'feeling safe because she had only recently started in the school' and because 'it was a very good department'. Curiously, Fiona Ingles, who was in her first year of teaching English, had also experienced an HMI inspection at a school in which she was doing her teaching practice during her PGCE year.

Both Helen and Fiona had also undergone appraisal at the school, which inevitably involved some classroom observation, and felt very comfortable with that process. A review of the English department, which involved classroom visits and scrutiny of documentation and a written report, had also been conducted by Mavis Bentley some 12 months previously as part of the school's ongoing curriculum review process. This had identified a number of targets for the English department.

In many ways, then, the English department at St Augustine's was well prepared for an OFSTED inspection. It is, perhaps, of incidental interest that the school's chair of governors is himself a lay inspector.

Dramatis personae

Mavis Bentley – deputy headteacher (24 years teaching experience, 11 of them as deputy headteacher at St Augustine's High School).
Helen Roberts – head of English (20 years teaching experience, four

as head of English).

Fiona Ingles – English teacher (two terms teaching experience).

Jack Eliot – English inspector (22 years teaching experience ending as head of English, 11 years as LEA English inspector).

Before the inspection

The announcement of the new OFSTED system, therefore, was regarded in a positive light by Mavis Bentley. However, she admitted to feeling 'a bit of concern at first, natural human concern that somewhere you value, the school you work in' was going to be inspected and 'you wonder if you'll fall short'. 'Having gone through our previous inspection,' she said, 'there were things we knew needed doing and it would help us do them quicker.' However, she admitted to some trepidation on hearing that St Augustine's was to be inspected during the first year of the new system, although she felt it was best 'to get on with it, get it over and done with'. The school suffered a little from some bad press coverage at the time because:

> What happened was that the newspapers got hold of the fact that we were going to be inspected, which was no problem because there were a number of other schools in the area. But they put it in with a statement that schools that were causing concern were due to be inspected in the first year.

Helen Roberts, on the other hand, did not take such a positive view initially. She recalls 'laughing with cynicism' at what she saw was 'another attack upon teachers' and 'feeling that people would be watching us who knew nothing about teaching and had a political agenda'. Fiona Ingles was still at university, concentrating on her PGCE work and has no recall of the announcement.

The school was disappointed at first that the LEA inspectorate did not win the contract; instead the contract for inspection went to an independent team. 'But at the same time we had always thought that someone with a Catholic bias would have got it', recalls Mavis Bentley, and, as it turned out, the registered inspector was a Catholic himself.

Helen Roberts, along with the rest of the staff, knew who was on the inspection team and their backgrounds because they were kept fully informed by senior management of the school 'so that the fears about people who knew nothing about education were gone'. She herself knew nothing of the person inspecting English, although she attended a meeting called by her LEA English inspector who knew the English inspector 'so he came recommended and I was able to go to the department and tell them that I knew personally people who thought that Jack Eliot was a good chap'. Fiona Ingles also had a view of the English inspector because 'he taught us for some sessions at the university' during her PGCE year and she passed her perceptions on to the rest of the English department. Mavis Bentley knew one other member of the inspection team, a former HMI who had visited the school some time previously and 'he had been very positively supportive'.

In order to 'dilute the fear' and to 'reduce the trepidation', the school invited the registered inspector to talk to the whole staff and to their Parents' Forum on the day he came to collect the pre-inspection documentation. The school also asked the LEA inspectorate to look at the documentation when they had got it ready to 'tell us how lacking it was' and that was felt, according to Mavis Bentley, to be 'a very positive move as well':

> They were quite extraordinarily good and I would recommend that to anyone. It was every bit of documentation we had done. They spent a day looking at it all.

Even though nothing was changed as a result of this scrutiny, Mavis Bentley felt that this 'gave us a lot more confidence'.

Other preparation by the school included the identification of responsibilities for senior staff according to the OFSTED *Framework for the Inspection of Schools*, meetings of senior management and of the policy group, weekly departmental meetings, pupil tracking within each year group and ability range by the deputy headteacher, after which she 'fed back to people what I actually thought of their lessons, honestly'. Mavis Bentley admitted that 'the general work of the school was led for six months by OFSTED' but still felt that this had been worthwhile.

Prior to the inspection, the senior management had decided to give more information about the curriculum to parents and had devised 'parent curriculum guides' during the previous year, which told parents succinctly 'what's done, when, where and how' and these were upgraded for the inspection. Departmental handbooks, many of which were 'only a couple of pages' previously, also were upgraded. Mavis Bentley was adamant that this upgrading of the school's documentation was well under way before the OFSTED inspection, 'what it enabled us to do was to do it much faster'.

Helen Roberts echoed this perception, recalling 'a more speedy writing down of developing practice'.

> By that stage I had pulled the rug from under the feet of the department and taken away many of the props that had been there and we were gradually replacing them. OFSTED speeded it up and made us formalise it. The docu-

mentation was a committing to paper of what was already happening. It was growing and living but, if anyone had come in and asked us to show what we were doing, we would have had to talk about it rather than show them the book.

Fiona Ingles felt the pressures of writing differently:

All my lessons had to be planned in detail and written down. It took me a long time.

As the inspection loomed closer, Mavis Bentley's greatest concern was the parents' meeting, because of her fear that 'parents come to school to complain'. Consequently, the school took steps to ensure that the parent governors, members of the PTA and representatives from the Parents' Forum attended that meeting.

Helen Robert's concerns were largely focused on one member of her department 'who had been in the habit of teaching in the style I really wanted to change' but who had already begun to operate in a much wider range of styles and 'we had laughed with and at' this teacher as 'the children doing drama spilled out of the classroom door'. This teacher needed a lot of reassurance beforehand 'not to draw the horns in and go back to what was felt safe but to stick with what was now being done'. Fiona was anxious because 'I didn't want to let the department down'.

At around this time, Jack Eliot, a former LEA English inspector who had retired some three years previously in order to write a novel, was beginning to scrutinise the departmental handbook and other information about the school which had been sent to him by the registered inspector. Jack too had felt very negative about the creation of OFSTED and felt:

It was a direct result of political notions of accountability and that agendas were being set which I wouldn't necessarily see as being directly relevant to the real needs of schools. And I didn't see that it would necessarily be an instrument for the improvement of schools. It was to do with something else. There would be clear decisions not to focus on certain things. And it would come up with evidence that could be manipulated to suit whatever was the political whim at the time.

Nevertheless he applied for training because 'in my particular circumstances I needed the work and that's all I could do!' He remembers his training week as being 'extremely hard work, not so much in the actual demands of the tasks but in the lack of time. In other words, I knew the answers but I hadn't got time to tell them.' But he didn't have any sense of being watched all the time and was very fulsome in praise of the HMI who led his group skilfully within the inevitable constraints of the assessment.

I couldn't care less if they were watching me in the bar. Remember, I was watching them too to see if they'd stand their corner!

Jack believes that it is possible to bring about improvements through inspection, although it is difficult. His initial perceptions were that 'opportunities for human discourse would be strictly limited' but his subsequent experience of inspections he has been involved in have shown that this is not the case, 'although the Framework doesn't make it easy'. However, he felt that the thinking behind the OFSTED system was that 'improvement is about measurable results' whereas he believes that 'it is nowhere as simple as that – improvement is a much wider and more complicated thing, isn't it?'

> None the less I do think you are in a position to have some impact on the style of teaching. In other words, what I thought might be just a very cold and distant process of observation and reporting, I don't think it is. It can be. And some people may be happy to keep it like that. But there are opportunities to bring about improvement in a much more general way. And part of that is to be able to recognise strengths and praise those strengths rather than simply identifying weaknesses, the correction of which will lead to better results.

Jack had no prior knowledge of St Augustine's. His first perceptions of the English department from the documents he received were that 'it looked well organised with some interesting features, such as the "Shakespeare in Schools" project'. He was interested that they had chosen the Welsh GCSE board for their pupils, that there was 'lots of mention of IT', and that drama was integrated within the curriculum. He also recalls that the examination results were very good, although there was 'some discrepancy between girls and boys in terms of their success and in the entry policies, particularly in literature, so that did raise questions about equality of opportunity'. However, his overview at this stage was that 'this was a department that was reading, and aware of developments, and thinking about how they could best serve their pupils'.

During the inspection

On the Monday morning of the inspection week Fiona Ingles was feeling very nervous because she felt that 'the life of the department depended on the inspection'. Helen Roberts remembers feeling 'terrified':

> I remember feeling sick and not being able to eat breakfast and yet there was a sense of excitement and relief – you know, thank God, at last it's arrived. It was a bit like going on stage where you know that you've prepared although you can't be absolutely certain that the scenery won't fall down. And the

adrenalin once you're on stage makes you perform and actually enjoy it. But it's when you're waiting in the wings, driving to school, that you actually need to get your feet in school first.

Mavis Bentley recalls 'being here very early but I'd got to the stage where I was feeling very positive', because she knew how much hard work had been put in by the staff and because 'we had been absolutely open and above board with the registered inspector and told him where the gaps were'. When the inspectors arrived and set about their work:

> I breathed a sigh of relief. I'd seen that the coffee was made. And it was down to them then. To that extent my job was finished. An absolute sigh of relief. I just had to make sure that everyone was in the right place at the right time and that was all.

Jack Eliot remembers feeling 'a bit rushed, a bit apprehensive about the whole process, knowing there was a lot to do in a very short time' and knew that he would be 'much happier once I get into a lesson – when I see some kids at work, I'll be alright'. This was the first OFSTED inspection he had done and he remembers vividly the desire to 'get into a classroom'.

Helen's first impression of Jack was that 'he seemed nice – he presented himself in a very quiet, unassuming, unaggressive way immediately and therefore he was not a "presence" in the classroom – he successfully became as much a fly on the wall as he was able to'. Jack too remembers having a good impression of Helen:

> She didn't seem to have any anxieties – I'm sure she did, but she seemed as relaxed as you could be in that kind of situation. So our meeting was very friendly, very relaxed. I felt I was talking to someone who had a tremendous amount of experience and was very open to other ideas and was very warm in actual fact. Her communication skills were very well developed. I didn't feel there were going to be any difficulties whatsoever. I felt as welcome as far as one can be. And there was a genuine desire to treat the experience as positively as possible.

Fiona's first contact with Jack came during the last lesson on the Monday afternoon when she was observed teaching a Year 8 class. Afterwards he commented to her that 'that was one of the best lessons on *Macbeth*' he had ever seen which made her feel much more comfortable and confident. She also recalls that 'nobody said what had been said about their lesson' in the staffroom at mid-morning break and lunch time and that 'people were quite closed about it all'. She was seen teaching on four separate occasions, twice with Year 8 classes, once with a Year 7 class during a tutorial period when the class were writing letters to one of their members who was in hospital, and once with a 'very lively' mixed-ability Year 9 class who were doing some drama work on Northern Ireland based on their reading of *Across the Barricades*. This latter lesson she recalls vividly because of the support she got from the pupils, who 'kept checking with me by whispering "Is that OK?" and "Do you think we'll be allowed to say bloody hell?"'. Again Jack Eliot's comments at the end of the lesson were positive and supportive.

Helen reported that some teachers felt 'very threatened' and some felt they had been 'grilled' by the inspector. This was particularly true, she thought, for Fiona, 'although by the end of the week it was obvious that the inspector was saying very nice things about her'. She herself did not think she had behaved any differently during lessons where she was observed:

> I think I behaved much the same as usual. The children would have let me know if I'd done anything different. Everything was much the same as usual but it was a performance because there's someone watching you. And also I was aware that the children were reacting slightly differently. Some of them were much less open and they clammed up while other classes were fine and quite relaxed.

According to Mavis Bentley, teachers adopted a range of strategies during the week of the inspection and many of them, she felt, played safe. Fiona Ingles's perception was that 'people did things that were out of the ordinary to some extent, because we wanted to show a lively department at its best'.

Consequently, in her view 'there was more drama, more speaking and listening than normal'. Helen Roberts pointed out that:

> We talked about it beforehand and we compared notes on what we were going to do. And certainly I wanted to encourage them as much as possible to do the best of what they would normally do, the best that was within their normal range. Because if they were to do anything unusual, it wouldn't work. And also because if the OFSTED report was to be of any value, then we ought to be presenting the best of what we normally did and seeing how we came out of it.

However, she did draw attention to 'two teachers who don't sleep at night when they know they are being visited the next day' and to her need to support them.

Jack had his own concerns because two other members of the inspection team had formerly been HMIs with responsibility for English, although in the end 'that worked quite well – there was no conflict, no clash of views at all'. He felt no difficulty about getting into classrooms, although he was aware of 'looking at a performance' at times. He also noted that:

Nearly all the lessons were to do with speaking and listening. I saw very little writing taking place although there was plenty of writing in folders and on display. I don't think that was a conscious decision, it would have been an odd one really. It was just the way it happened. There was a tremendous focus on speaking and listening.

This was in some ways inhibiting, particularly because he was unable to check out the apparent teacher inconsistencies in approaches to drafting and when it came to reporting back he had to leave that 'as a question because I didn't really have the evidence'. But otherwise Jack felt the department was trying to be 'as normal as they could be, although clearly they were nervous'. The children, he felt, were 'generally speaking quite relaxed – they were all prepared to talk to me and some would initiate conversation themselves'. This he put down to the fact that 'it was a department that was used to having lots of people in' and he noted their involvement with the Shakespeare in Schools project and with a Theatre in Education company.

As the inspection week drew to its close, Helen was preparing herself to receive Jack's oral report on English at St Augustine's. She remembers:

First of all, I would have been disappointed to be surprised by anything that was in the report. The actual process I was nervous about but then when I discovered that there was to be me, my headteacher as my support and scribe, Jack with his senior in the team as his witness, and then another HMI who was checking the whole process, then a sense of the ridiculous took over. I felt quite sorry for Jack with all that going on around him.

In preparing to give his report, Jack was aware of Helen as the major audience, since it was only just before the meeting that he discovered that there would be others present. There were no major criticisms 'and that always makes it easier', but he knew that he had to raise certain issues to do with gender matters, to do with the selection of resources and texts, to do with drafting, and to do with progression and continuity and 'didn't feel there was going to be any problem in doing so'. His major concern was 'to deliver a relatively coherent report in a short space of time', so he tried to make his report 'succinct', tried to 'allow time for Helen to comment' and also tried to 'ensure they got the praise they deserved as well as taking on the few areas for development'. He had also decided, because he knew there would be a member of senior management present, to draw the school's attention to the lack of a drama studio. However, he was determined to seek to provide opportunities to 'engage in a dialogue' with Helen Roberts as his main focus and didn't have time to worry about the other presences in the room.

Helen felt that she 'didn't only hear the criticisms' in Jack's report because she was 'very willing to hear the praise' in what she considered to be a very fair report. She went 'straight back to the department and gave them an oral feedback and I was able to give them a pat on the back, which allowed me to send them away happy at the end of the week'. There were one or two comments in the oral report which she felt did not acknowledge 'work that we had already started' and, having raised these, she was pleased that Jack took note of them and amended his comments on them in the final written version. Fiona Ingles, one of the recipients of Helen's oral feedback, was 'pleased because the department was good', particularly when she found through conversation with other teachers in the school that 'English was better than other departments'.

After the inspection

At the end of the inspection week Helen Roberts felt 'pleased, exhausted, drained'; Fiona Ingles had 'a sense of relief that it was over'; Mavis Bentley also felt 'tired but in the main positive'. Jack Eliot thought his first OFSTED inspection had been 'a good experience' because of the leadership of the registered inspector who 'was very well organised, made me feel very welcome, and shared his anxieties, and had a sense of humour'. However, he admitted to 'a sense of relief', particularly after the two evening meetings which lasted until very late. The registered inspector himself was 'worried about the lateness of the meetings and kept asking "How can I do it better?"'.

When the registered inspector returned over a week later to read his draft report to the senior management team, Mavis Bentley, who had sought to be supportive of all the departmental heads during the subject feedbacks in the inspection week, felt 'terribly vulnerable':

That was the time I felt bad, because the criticisms were levelled at me. And it was the headteacher who had to keep the balance. All of a sudden the roles were reversed. I was keeping the balance during the heads of department feedbacks but now he had to keep it. In spite of all the documentation, which they said was very good, what they really wanted and everyone should know this, what they are really looking at is the quality of teaching and learning. And that is what they are inspecting. And all the documentation will say is that this is a well-managed school. During that week they are looking at the quality of teaching and learning and that is not down to you, it's down to every member of staff that they observe.

When the written report arrived some weeks later, it was distributed to all the staff. The section on English, written by Jack Eliot, praises the standards achieved in speaking and listening, reading, and writing, commends the 'good working relationships' maintained by teachers and the 'consistently high standard' of the department's assessment procedures. Although the report stresses that 'in the majority of lessons pupils were well motivated, collaborated well together and took great care in the presentation of their work', concern is expressed about some 'undemanding parameters' within which lower-ability sets operated and to the uneven gender balance of some teaching groups.

Helen Roberts was rather disappointed because 'the oral report had been, because there was a personal element in it, more warmly full of praise'. The report, she felt, overall 'was a fair reflection but on balance I think the warmth had gone from it'. The English department all read the report, remembers Fiona Ingles, but Helen Roberts had to point them to other parts of the report where English featured, as well as the specific subject paragraphs.

The school did not wait for the publication of the report before beginning to take action. Notes taken by members of the senior management from the oral reports to heads of department were typed up and circulated, together with a school pro-forma requiring each department to identify positive statements and statements for improvement in the report on their subject, and to outline plans for addressing each of these areas for improvement, with time scales and key staff identified. This was then returned to the headteacher. Helen Roberts told what happened next:

> And we're now gradually trying to work our way through. Some of it we've certainly met. Some of it has been slower than I would have liked.

The actions agreed by each department were then translated into the whole-school curriculum plan. A training day was used to deal with whole-school issues, such as differentiation and equal opportunities. Two of the training days in the following year are to be spent with the LEA English inspector 'who we still regard as our adviser' working in school alongside the staff.

Final perceptions

Fiona Ingles – English teacher
It was very good in bringing everyone together to ensure we were doing common work. In the end it was a fair assessment and it certainly was not a pointless exercise. I also had some feedback from another inspector who had interviewed some Year 11 pupils who had

told her how much they enjoyed English. I was really surprised to receive this, but really pleased to know they appreciated the work I'd put in to help them.

Helen Roberts – head of English
I hate to say this but the National Curriculum gave me the springboard I needed to work with the department, so that OFSTED confirmed and re-affirmed that direction. When we saw some of the paperwork that the inspectors would be using, when we saw that they would definitely be looking for different teaching styles, it was then obvious to the department that the different styles we had been working towards in answer to the National Curriculum would be required for this. The inspection pushed the accelerator down. The department afterwards felt very secure that the paths that were being trod were definitely OK. So it gave confidence. I went home very happy.

Mavis Bentley – deputy headteacher
It was very positive. It accelerated things that we were already doing. There was nothing that was unexpected, which we were grateful for. But then again, if you identify your weaknesses, then people will... I shan't say any more.

Jack Eliot – English inspector
I've always believed that inspection can help and my experience of that is being involved in LEA reviews, as we called them rather than inspections. But I know there was a very different structure. They were designed to help and therefore they were structured in a very different way. But I do feel that, although it's not as easy because there are a different set of procedures, there is sufficient flexibility within that to help. But if you were to do it almost to the letter of the law – and I've seen people do it – then I don't think that is going to help very much. A lot of it depends, as it always will I suppose, on the response of the school and actually also on the attitude of the inspection team. If you feel like you're ploughing a lonely furrow, maybe you're less likely to feel you are part of a helpful process.

Postscript

Some weeks after the OFSTED inspection of St Augustine's, Helen Roberts was asked by her LEA English inspector to address an audience of heads of English from elsewhere in the county about her experiences.

She recalls this as follows:

There were 50 or 60 faces sitting in front of me. And I looked at them and I suddenly remembered 'That's how I felt'. And it was very cathartic, because although it was some weeks afterwards I suddenly realised that I was still quite hyped up after it. And that talking to them and realising how nervous they were made me feel...well, I've talked about it, I've had the catharsis, I've put it behind me. The adrenalin that was still lingering finally stopped at that point. I hadn't realised that I was still feeling slightly tense about it.

CHAPTER 4

N is for Knackered: Newton Middle School (9–13)

Background

Newton Middle School had recently assumed grant-maintained status, when the contract for inspection of the school was awarded to its former LEA's inspectorate. An inevitable tension was thus created. The Standing Committee on Grant-Maintained Schools, acting on behalf of Newton Middle School and five other grant-maintained schools in a similar situation, held discussions with barristers in chambers in London to consider the possibility of taking the matter to judicial review. In the end, the Standing Committee pulled back from this position when it was given assurances by Professor Stuart Sutherland, HMCI, that particular concerns would be looked at individually, that each inspection of a grant-maintained school in this situation would be monitored by HMI, and that it was possible for them to challenge the inspection team membership under the legislation.

Newton Middle School itself is part of the three-tier education system created by its southern county LEA after local government reorganisation in 1974. It was a new school then, built to serve the growing population of a small town on the fringes of a large metropolitan area which had been designated a New Town. The small market town, which had had a steady population of 20000 people for the greater part of this century, saw itself growing at an alarming rate during the 1960s and 1970s as central government pumped money into supporting new housing developments designed to take the pressures off the metropolis. By the 1990s, growth had more or less ceased and the population had stabilised at around 150 000 people. Such population movements, of course, have their costs, uprooting large numbers of people from traditional patterns of urban life and transporting them into new situations where patterns of life have to be created almost from nothing. This is particularly true for family life, where the sort of extended families common to stable communities are rarely possible in such New Towns.

Newton Middle School serves such an area. Its pupil population, which covers the age range from nine to 13, comes in the main from two neighbouring first schools, with a small number coming from a variety of other schools in the surrounding district. The children come from a range of socio-economic backgrounds, although this is skewed to the more middle-class end of the scale. 12 per cent of pupils are eligible for free school meals and there are only two pupils with statements of special educational need. 4 per cent of the 550 pupils are members of ethnic minorities. The majority of pupils transfer at 13 to the neighbouring high school.

Dramatis personae

Francis Johnston – headteacher (24 years teaching experience, including 15 years as headteacher).
Alice Walker – head of English (26 years teaching experience, 16 of them at Newton Middle School though only two as head of English).
Brenda Royce – class teacher (14 years teaching experience, five of them at Newton Middle School).
Matthew Dickens – English inspector (23 years teaching experience ending as head of English in a secondary school, five years as LEA English inspector).

Before the inspection

Headteacher Francis Johnston was in his second headteacher post at the time of the OFSTED inspection. He had been at Newton Middle School for eight years and in both his headships he had had experience of short HMI inspections and of LEA inspections. The latter he regarded with some scepticism, since their quality had been variable, although he had a particularly high regard for the specialist middle school inspector of his ex-LEA. He had, however, been very impressed with the quality of the experiences undergone during the HMI visits to his school immediately prior to its becoming grant-maintained.

Although he himself did not find inspections difficult, he admitted to being 'shell-shocked' when he heard that his school was to be inspected during the first year 'because it had been a strenuous year having just become a grant-maintained school, with a fairly difficult departure from the LEA, and we were hoping to catch our breath'. Consequently, because of the peculiarity of the situation described earlier and because he felt that 'the parents are entitled to an objective view of the school', Francis Johnston felt he had to state his position:

> When I met the registered inspector, I made it clear that the governors had been concerned and that legal advice had been sought. I felt that was quite enough to ensure that we had a fair inspection.

Matthew Dickens, the LEA's English inspector who was part of the team that inspected Newton Middle School, remembers first hearing about this from his team leader:

> I found it offensive that the school had sought legal advice, because it suggested that we were incompetent and incapable of setting on one side any feelings about whether it was grant-maintained or not. We had passed the OFSTED training and we could do the job. I suppose the waters were muddied by the government through its various white papers trying to erect this Chinese wall between inspection and advice, and this odd notion of 'contamination' that had arisen. I certainly think that as a team we were and are professional enough to set aside our personal views and do the job properly.

Matthew Dickens was also concerned about the establishment of the OFSTED system because 'it was interfering with the development of a repertoire of LEA inspections which had a developmental thrust', some of which were still continuing. For instance, there was a rolling programme of visits to secondary school departments which he felt were much more useful and manageable for the schools and didn't 'create a state of institutional jitter'. Nevertheless, his LEA had encouraged all of its inspectors to apply for OFSTED training and Matthew himself was accepted for one of the early training weeks. He remembers it vividly:

> It was initially one of the most disturbing experiences I can remember. I felt physically sick, emotionally and professionally very discomfited. I think that says more about me than about the process. I don't imagine people deliberately set out to make you feel like that. And I did feel a lot better by day two because I had then established there was a community of suffering. But I thought it was appalling. It may be scrupulously fair because everybody's treated alike but you could treat everybody very badly and justify

it on the grounds that it was fair. It was inhumane. It was the fail/pass bit. If you failed your training, what would you do with your life? It was appalling.

He is not convinced that a judgemental inspection system where the strengths and weaknesses in a school 'are identified by a bunch of strangers who then disappear' would necessarily lead to improvement. He also feels it is very much up to the attitude of the school as to whether the exercise was beneficial and knew himself of one headteacher within his LEA who referred to his school's OFSTED inspection as '£20 000 of free INSET'. This was a school, thought Matthew, 'which was genuinely pleased to have its practice stretched, its principles examined and thrown back to them'. He is also concerned as to why the Subject Evidence Forms, which form the basis for most inspectors of their oral feedback on their subject, were 'secret documents'.

Alice Walker, the head of English at Newton Middle School, had been inspected as part of a HMI inspection 20 years previously, an experience she recalls as being stressful because she felt she was being inspected personally and the process was very anonymous. On hearing that her present school was to be inspected, her first reaction was that:

> It was a bit nerve-racking because it was so new. We were in the first wave and we had no experience to draw on. There were no colleagues who had already gone through it. It was the fear of the unknown. And there was the idea in the press that it was very much a policing thing and they'd be looking for the holes.

Brenda Royce, a class teacher in the school who had only returned to teaching full-time three years previously having had time working in a part-time capacity at the school while her children were young, had had no prior experience of inspections. When she heard that Newton Middle School was to be inspected, her reaction was one of 'considerable trepidation' because she 'imagined it would be like HMI inspections – pretty horrific'. She was also aware that the grant-maintained situation could 'be a cause of potential difficulty because we hadn't left the LEA on particularly amicable terms'.

There was, therefore, all the potential for this inspection to be a particularly stressful experience, partly because of the situation concerning the school and the LEA but also because of the attitudes, prior experiences and beliefs of some of the major participants.

In order to prepare themselves for the inspection, the school invited an inspector from a neighbouring LEA from whom in-service support was now being bought, to talk to the whole staff about the OFSTED inspection process, which helped in the demystification. A preliminary visit to the school by the registered inspector to talk to the staff helped further to reduce anxieties. An extensive programme of lesson observations was set up by Francis Johnston because 'some of them had never had an individual apart from me in their classroom for years and years'. These classroom observations, carried out using the OFSTED Lesson Observation Pro-forma, were conducted by all staff observing each other teaching and 'sharing the results of that observation with each other'. In terms of subject departments, Francis Johnston saw every head of department individually and 'looked at the relevant part of the *Framework for Inspection* in terms of their subject':

> I then asked them to go away and conduct a SWAT analysis of their own department and to come back and discuss that with me. Regardless of what state their schemes of work were in, they were all asked to review them. In every case, whether they were very good documents or not, we reproduced them, had them retyped and rebound, so the presentation was improved.

Brenda Royce recalls the classroom observation as being of particular value because 'it gave you the opportunity to see the kind of format the inspectors' notes would be taken in and what exactly they were looking for'. Much of the documentation she felt was already in place but she remembers:

> There seemed to be such a tremendous emphasis on the paperwork that people were rushing around madly trying to get everything prettied up, I suppose, presented, updated.

Alice Walker also attended talks at a nearby university given by a former HMI which 'put my mind at rest because now I knew the format, now I knew that I could challenge information that was inaccurate, and that there was going to be a two-way process'. She also knew Matthew Dickens slightly through attendance on courses and through her time on a short secondment from school on the LINC Project and was pleased that 'I was going to be inspected by someone who was an English specialist':

> I wanted to ensure that the department weren't worried about it. So I tried to reassure them actually that they were doing the right things and that, if they continued to do what they were doing, they wouldn't have a problem. And we discussed the kind of things they were going to be doing during that time, because it was the start of a new area in the half term.

The departmental documentation had been written at the end of the previous year after a visit by another member of the LEA's inspectorate to the school. Alice recalls that:

> He was very pleased with what he saw but I hadn't got anything down on paper because I'd only been in post a year and I didn't want to impose

anything on anybody. If people were going to make it work, they had to have ownership of it. So at the end of the year, after we'd evaluated each term's work, I wrote it all down.

She felt, therefore, that she was fortunate in being in this position and there was little need for her to do anything other than tidy up what was already in existence. She was, however, concerned about the recording of children's progress which 'had not been resolved beforehand'. She also 'went through work with lots of colleagues' to reassure them, which Brenda particularly found to be helpful. Brenda Royce was still feeling anxious going into the inspection because 'I had never been observed teaching since I came out of college' and 'although I felt I was doing the best I could, I was still quite nervous that I wouldn't be up to standard'. Like many of their colleagues, Brenda and Alice spent a large part of their half-term holiday in school preparing for the inspection, which commenced in the week immediately following half term.

Francis Johnston's concerns going into the inspection were the 'normal concerns of managing a school and having up to 13 other people wandering about'. He was also concerned that 'one or two of the LEA inspectors had particular prejudices in certain subject areas that we didn't agree with' and wondered how that would turn out. Though he was confident in his school, he was aware of having to support members of staff who would not cope with pressure very well. He felt he ran a very good school with a lot of competent and hard-working staff and wondered if the OFSTED inspection would be 'a snapshot that reflected what I thought was a very good school – there was an element of pot luck, an element of roulette in it'.

During the inspection

On the first day of the inspection week, the only one of the trio observed was Brenda Royce who was seen twice teaching French. She had arrived at school feeling very apprehensive:

> I was very, very stressed, particularly because it was French and I had to conduct it in the target language. So I battled on against all odds. I think perhaps you go for overkill really. I should have taken the opportunity to go into English because the children couldn't understand what I was saying and they were trying to keep going in French. But the French inspector was extremely good and perhaps went against the guidelines of OFSTED in that she did give some feedback at the end of the lesson, she was positively critical.

Alice Walker wondered when the lesson observations would begin for her and was sorry that Matthew Dickens would not be starting his inspection of English until the second day 'because at the beginning of the week I tend to introduce a new element and then the next two lessons are follow-ups of that element, so in fact the introductions were never seen by anybody'.

Having greeted the registered inspector and given the inspection team packs explaining the routines of the school, Francis Johnston felt that the first day was very long:

> It happened all round me as a head. I wasn't particularly involved. I spent great big chunks of that day supporting people and trying to find out how it was going. I wasn't observed, nobody interviewed me on that day. We had a policy of telling staff to give consistent feedback during the week. I depended on my two deputies and a senior teacher to come and tell me.

The early gossip in the staffroom was largely of the 'Have you been done yet?' variety, as Brenda Royce recalls, or 'Who's had who?', according to Alice Walker, and that 'inspectors were being as nice as they could be'. However, Brenda recalls noting that other teachers had not received the sort of feedback that she had from the French inspector.

Matthew Dickens, arriving at the school on the Tuesday morning, remembers feeling 'anxious about being on time and having the right bits of paper' but, as he also observed:

> You always feel a bit nervous and teachers are bemused when you share that with them. They think the anxiety and the stress is all on their side. I think it can be helpful to say that it can be quite stressful on you too. I think it's got a lot to do with spending your working day with people you don't know, so you're constantly going into rooms where there are 30 people you have never met before, stressed because you're there. You know that you're the cause of the stress and I think that makes you stressed and anxious if you're a reasonable human being, because you don't want to be the cause of stress and anxiety. But also the stress of knowing that you've got to do a hell of a lot of work in a very short space of time and you've got to get it right and, if you don't, it does matter because it's a very personal area you're working in and people can be very disturbed by judgements you make.

Matthew spent the greater part of Tuesday and Wednesday observing lessons, many of them taught by Alice Walker. Although they didn't spend time talking to each other during that first day, he 'sought her out early on' and remembers that his early perceptions, based on his reading of the impressive English documentation, were confirmed by 'some very enjoyable and effective lessons that she was responsible for'. Although she felt quite comfortable in general, she remembers one lesson particularly where:

I nearly lost my nerve half way through. I had decided I was going to teach as I normally taught, I was not going to do any specially prepared lessons, the all-singing all-dancing sort. But I had one lesson with a fast group in Years 7 and 8 and they're very able children and they had been writing their own short stories and we had organised before half term that they were going to read their short stories. And in fact we spent the whole lesson, which was 55 minutes, listening to three short stories. The quality of the work and the quality of the listening was absolutely superb. As an English teacher, I was absolutely thrilled with it because it was doing exactly what I wanted it to do. But then I thought if I was actually observing this lesson, would there have been enough variety? Would there have been enough pace? And I nearly lost my nerve then.

Matthew recalls the same lesson very well because:

I cried because the kids were so wonderful. I can't remember the piece, except that it made me cry. A child read some homework, just read some homework, a story, aloud to the class. And it was really very moving, very affecting.

In general, however, he found it easier to observe in lessons which were 'varied and active' and recalls an IT lesson where it was particularly easy to observe learning taking place. Sometimes he felt that Alice Walker 'used me, in the nicest possible way' by inviting children to read something again or show some work to 'the inspector'. He also feels that the notion of participant observer is not an impossible one, although 'there are limits, of course, because you can have a lot of fun and really get involved but you couldn't do the inspection job':

I know you're not meant to influence the conduct of the lesson and that participating in a sense is not on. It's a delicate business but I'm fairly happy that I can make the right type of judgements. I do think that being totally removed from the cut and thrust of the classroom, especially a good English classroom, is not possible.

The most stressful part of the whole inspection for Alice Walker was the two-hour meeting she had with Matthew Dickens after school on the Wednesday afternoon looking together at the departmental documentation:

It happened to be a day when I teach all day and I'm also on duty, so I hadn't had a break. The thing that struck me was that you do have to be very careful about what you say and how you say it. He was very pleasant and very nice, he was not threatening in any way. But, when you're tired and you're having to weigh every word, it's not easy. It started off beautifully. He said, 'This is a very good document. Can I keep it?' And then he went through it and it came across to me that he was looking for any holes. For example, I've got in my document about making sure there's no discrimination in terms of race and that sort of thing and we do teach that in Year 7 through bullying and *The Diary of Anne Frank* and things like that. But he wanted more written down and I just didn't understand how I could do it any more than that. What else could I do to point the way for people?

During his four days in the school Matthew Dickens was able to see a range of English teaching, though he recalls that he 'couldn't see everyone teaching English at Key Stage 2', which hampered his ability to make judgements on the whole school. Inevitably, in a middle school such as this, many of the teachers are not subject specialists but Brenda Royce was sure that most of her colleagues accepted the advice that was given to them beforehand that they 'would be very silly not to make sure that lessons were the best that they were capable of'. 'At the end of the day I think they saw a performance', she added, although she was surprised that 'one or two people showed little concern', even though these were temporary members of staff.

Alice Walker, on the other hand, felt that some of her colleagues had played safe, while others tried to do things they had never done before. She recalls having to support one teacher who 'tried to fit her lesson to the pro-forma by starting with one thing, after 15 minutes changing to another thing, after a further 15 minutes changing to another thing, instead of it flowing'. This teacher, normally a very capable person, was 'desperately trying to give the variety which she thought was necessary'. Her own attitude was, 'I'm doing the very best I can. There are always things I can learn but I would expect people to notice the good things as well, and I tried to say that to the rest of the staff.'

Matthew Dickens sensed that the staff of the school wanted 'the kids and the school and themselves to be seen in the best light' and felt that 'people had been put on their mettle' by the inspection process. He quoted an analogy which he had heard from elsewhere:

> When you invite someone to dinner, you don't have new carpets put down but you do vacuum the one you've got.

His impression of Newton Middle School staff was that 'they had vacuumed the carpet and that's a perfectly proper thing to do'.

Approaching the Friday morning when he was to present his oral report to Alice Walker, Matthew was aware of a 'complex bundle of aims' because:

> 'I wanted to get it right by the book but it also had to be a positive experience for the person on the receiving end, so you've got to try very hard to express things in sentences which are clear and unambiguous and you've got to try to sense the balance between the positives and the negatives.

Alice, having gone home in some distress on the Wednesday evening after her long meeting, thought that she had 'blown it':

> I'd actually picked up totally the wrong messages, you see. And maybe that's because I was tired. Even on the Friday I still wasn't absolutely sure that it would be OK. I was so nervous before I went in.

Brenda Royce had no worries and expected the report to be good 'because English is a strength of the school'. Headteacher Francis Johnston also had no qualms because he knew Alice to be 'a very good head of department'.

In the event, the oral report on English was in line with the school's expectations. Matthew recalls that 'I quite enjoyed the experience. If it's a good message, it's a pleasure to deliver it.' Alice too recalls the experience as being 'very positive in general, so I needn't have worried':

> I did feel it was fair. I mean, there are terms like satisfactory or above which... I think I'd expected the worst and it wasn't like that at all. It was fair, apart from the race and gender bit, but the thing is you don't think about that at the time. I felt that was quite small, it didn't really matter. But then later you think I wonder how he might have suggested I dealt with it, you know.

After the inspection

The general feeling at Newton Middle School at the end of the inspection week was one of 'exhaustion'. Alice Walker felt 'relief that it was all over' and remembers that there was a lot of mutual support among the staff. Brenda Royce remembers that 'some of the Key Stage 2 teachers felt that Key Stage 2 hadn't come out as well as Key Stage 3 and they felt hurt by that'.

Francis Johnston received 'no clues on the whole school at the end of the week – I had to make my judgements based on staff comment and reaction'. He and his deputies had attended all of the subject feedbacks, however. He had some concerns at the end of the week that in general terms 'they might not have got an accurate view of the school'.

The formal reading of the draft report by the registered inspector occurred some three weeks later. Francis Johnston and his deputies, with a secretary to take shorthand, attended this report reading session. He recalls:

> I listened to it all but you don't really hear it. I was in defence mode. I had made the point that right up until the written report I would take every possible opportunity, no matter how marginal, to improve the writing of the report. In theory, all that the session was for was to correct factual

inaccuracies. I corrected several factual inaccuracies and I attempted to influence the way the report was written. I didn't hear the nice things. I just corrected. Every time I listened and heard something that I thought was not fair, was not accurate, I made a comment. At the end, I think they were very disappointed that I wasn't saying thank you very much, that's a great report.

The published report on English, written by Matthew Dickens, includes the following very positive statements in its introductory paragraph:

Most pupils speak with clarity and confidence. They write with increasing fluency and accuracy, making good use of the drafting process. Some outstandingly good writing is produced in Years 7 and 8 where some pupils have also acquired sophisticated word-processing skills. At all levels pupils are successfully encouraged to read widely from a progressively demanding range of texts.

The only hint of criticism is in the statement that 'non-specialist teachers would benefit from more detailed documentation on marking, on the teaching of drama and on the use of texts which raise equal opportunity issues'.

When the report arrived, Alice Walker felt that 'the sense hadn't changed' since the oral feedback and 'there were lots of very positive comments throughout the report about English teaching, not just in the English section'. Brenda Royce was 'very pleased with the French and the English', although she felt that the Key Stage 2 teachers had been judged 'a little harshly', which she put down to the fact that, for the purposes of the OFSTED inspection, Newton Middle School had been regarded as a secondary school and that this model of inspection worked less satisfactorily in the earlier years of her school – a view echoed by Matthew Dickens.

Francis Johnston, however, was rather disappointed with the final written version, although 'they found little wrong with the school' and 'it was a positive report'. As he had done with every other aspect of the inspection, however, he set about managing parental reaction to the report. Through the school's weekly newsletter, he had kept parents informed before, during and after the inspection, including his concerns about the LEA team winning the inspection contract. In one newsletter he reported on the registered inspector's report to the governing body and, after quoting statistics about standards of achievement, the quality of learning and the quality of teaching, he wrote, 'These figures would place Newton Middle School in a very high position in any national league'. Interestingly, this was picked up by a local newspaper which reported that OFSTED said the school 'would be placed very high in any national league'.

The school is still in the process of addressing the findings of the OFSTED report. An Action Plan has been prepared by senior management and governors which outlines the school's intentions for addressing each of the key issues identified in the report. Heads of department are reviewing their work in the light of comments made on their subjects. Alice Walker has had discussions with staff towards achieving greater uniformity in marking and has subsequently presented a draft policy document to the whole staff for further discussion. The school buys support to help teachers in their reviews from a range of providers – 'anywhere there is good advice and support available', according to Francis Johnston, and is considering buying some services from its former LEA.

Final perceptions

Francis Johnston – headteacher
I hope it stays in roughly the same format. I think it will improve standards. I disagree with fellow headteachers who are critical of the whole set-up. I learned something new about my school. The inspection put certain internal perceptions into a framework. It also affirmed the positive and celebrated the achievements of the school. Interestingly a number of staff were still making positive comments about the experience several weeks later. In some departments, it has improved attitudes. And I think we are all aware of the next time round.

Brenda Royce – class teacher
I'm tempted to say it's been a huge waste of money. I think it has been of value to the school for publicity purposes, because we've obviously apparently done very well and our reputation has spread in the area as being a good school. And that can only be of value in that respect. Personally, I didn't find it of any value to me. I found the whole thing very stressful. We all came together very well as a staff, which was a positive. When I heard that so many per cent of lessons were satisfactory or above, I knew mathematically I couldn't have fallen into a category that was unsatisfactory. So I knew I must have been reasonable. I think I was fairly confident about myself until I knew that somebody was going to come in and look at me.

Matthew Dickens – English inspector
It's hard for me to know, because I'm at the wrong end. I think you

have to ask the schools and I think you'll get a whole variety of answers. It comes back to this basic business of a school's attitude towards it and whether they're prepared to see it as something useful or not. I'm suspicious about Action Plans but I've no real knowledge of what Action Plans mean in practice. And the key points are generally so broad that from a subject point of view I doubt whether the Action Plans mean very much. But I've had some evidence that some departments have picked up their feedback and used it to carry their practice forward. Some departments have sharpened up their act as a result of being threatened with an inspection. So I think it is contributing in some ways to the development of practice, inevitably, but from a subject point of view we could achieve more without this cradle-to-grave once-every-four-years approach. I think it's a very crude measure.

Alice Walker – head of English
I think it's a very expensive way of checking up on schools and I'd be very surprised if they can keep it going, particularly with all the cuts that they want to make. But on the other hand it does focus the mind. There were lots of things where I kept thinking, 'I must get that done'. And it never comes to the top of the list because there are other more pressing everyday things. But, when you've suddenly got this, then it has to come to the top of the list. But most of us were in school most of the summer and most of half term, so as a result we've all been very tired this academic year. And our parents are very supportive and they would have lynched the inspectors if we'd had a bad report. But I would worry about the schools that are not as fortunate. I can think of some schools where people are all pulling against each other. They'd go under in an OFSTED inspection. And it did bring us closer together as a staff. We laughed so much! In one English lesson there was one wonderful teacher who was trying to get the children to think of some really interesting words describing a tree and she said, 'Think of a word that begins with 'n' and one of the kids said, 'Knackered, miss!' And everyone, the inspector as well, fell about laughing.

CHAPTER 5

The Nightmare Scenario: Sheriff High School (11–18)

Background

Sheriff High School is a former grammar school, in which guise it had a long and distinguished history, as the honours boards around the entrance hall and some of its older buildings, one of which is Grade 2 listed, make clear. The school, now comprehensive, is situated in the East Midlands and draws its pupils from five surrounding villages. These villages developed as largely coal-mining areas but the pits closed some 20 years ago and there is now a variety of light and manufacturing industries in the area. The school draws its pupils from households across the social spectrum and, in many ways, its catchment area is broadly typical of the country in terms of social class, according to census reports. However, this disguises the fact that two of the villages, which lie at the extremity of the catchment area, contain significant levels of socio-economic deprivation, with a considerable number of homes having no-one in full-time employment.

Quite a low proportion of pupils, 9 per cent, were at the time of the OFSTED inspection entitled to free school meals. However, an above average number of pupils were in receipt of statements of special educational need. At the time of the inspection this number was 21, though others were awaiting assessment. A reading test administered by the school to pupils on entry suggests that the intake leans heavily towards the lower end of the academic ability range.

The school teaches pupils between the ages of 11 and 18 and has just under 1000 on roll, with numbers greater at the lower end of the school than in Years 10 and 11. Currently, just over half of its pupils stay at the school for post-16 education, where they are joined by a small number from neighbouring 11–16 schools. Well over half of the sixth form proceed to higher education of one sort or another. Examination results at both GCSE and A level are below national figures, although the reverse is true in English.

Roy Adler had come as headteacher to Sheriff High some 18 months prior to the inspection. He had for seven years previously been headteacher of a comprehensive school in the south of England, so it was fairly early in his tenure of office at Sheriff High that he heard that he was to receive an OFSTED inspection. He recalls:

> A certain amount of dread, to be honest, but I think slight pleasure that it was earlier than it might have been and not so far into my headship that I couldn't use it to bring further the changes that by this time I knew needed to happen. So it was quite a useful timing actually. If it's too soon then you haven't had time to look at the school yourself; several years in and you're entirely to blame for what's happening.

Initially sceptical of the whole OFSTED process, which he saw as 'another government intrusion on schools which have by and large been very successful in looking after themselves', he himself had only one previous experience of a school inspection. This was when he had been a head of department in a school which received a full inspection from its LEA inspectorate 'because it was in a management mess'. He recalls his own experience of being observed teaching during this inspection as being 'fairly stressful' and the whole process as being 'rather harsh but it needed doing for the school's sake'. The headteacher of that school 'subsequently retired, which was presumably the point of the exercise'.

Head of English Don Meadows, by contrast, who had been at Sheriff High for the whole 17 years of his teaching career, the last four of these as head of department, had experienced four HMI inspections during his time, as well as visits to his lesson by the LEA English adviser. All of these inspection visits to his classroom had been positive 'despite my worries beforehand', although he recalls that one inspector 'was not as positive in his manner' as others had been. The announcement of the creation of OFSTED he greeted as:

> First of all something to be suspicious of. I didn't – and don't – have any trust in the government's motivation behind things. I had respect for the old HMI system. And I saw this as another bit of the privatisation process. So that would have been another thing to bash teachers with. Although I do agree that schools have got to be inspected and, as a parent, I think it's a good thing.

On hearing that Sheriff High was to be in the first round of inspections, he felt 'quite relieved' that he knew when it was going to be and, since he had been in post as head of English for four years, 'in a way I wanted to be inspected, not with great delight, but it is quite useful for people to see if things are going along alright'.

His colleague and second in department, Angela Smith, had missed a proportion of the previous year while supporting her husband, who was also on the staff of the school, during his fatal illness. She had been teaching for the same length of time as Don Meadows but had no prior experience of inspections. Her first reaction on hearing that Sheriff High was to have an OFSTED inspection was 'Oh no, not something else! What's it going to be like? What do they want? Who are they?'

Both Angela and Don had been appraised during the previous year by a colleague from the English department, in line with the school's peer-appraisal system and both had felt quite comfortable with the classroom observation element of that because of knowing the colleague who was appraising.

Janet Woolf, who conducted the inspection of English at Sheriff High School, had herself experienced a lot of classroom observation as a teacher. She had been involved in two HMI inspections and had several 'less formal LEA inspectors' visits and observations'. She recalls being 'faintly nervous the first time an inspector watched me teach' but in general she 'found the experience stimulating'. The second full HMI inspection occurred when:

> I was an established, confident head of department with a very able team of teachers; I knew that all was well before they came. I gained advice from them about record-keeping which was helpful.

The regular classroom observation that she had experienced arose because her department was often the subject of inter-LEA research, which attracted other heads of English to visit her school 'to see how we organised and taught and gained successful results in what was generally acknowledged to be a tough school'. One of the interesting features of her department was its mentoring system in which:

> Every teacher observed and judged another's performance. We watched each other a great deal, in an open, honest atmosphere. I was sometimes the subject of criticism by teachers who had taught longer than I had and by those who had only recently qualified. It was always useful, often enjoyable, occasionally painful.

So, for Janet Woolf, being observed by a fellow professional in the classroom was 'never a nerve-wracking experience' because 'like many English teachers I enjoy performing'. However, having had experience of running her school's training programme and subsequently of helping teachers in difficulty in her LEA, 'I know that many teachers hate and fear observation and I feel sympathy for them'.

There were, therefore, quite varied experiences and perceptions, particularly of classroom observation, going into the OFSTED inspection.

Dramatis personae

Roy Adler – headteacher (26 years teaching experience, including nine as headteacher).

Don Meadows – head of English (17 years teaching experience, all at Sheriff High School, including four as head of English).

Angela Smith – second in English department (17 years teaching experience).

Janet Woolf – English inspector (27 years teaching experience ending as head of English, three years as advisory teacher for English).

Before the inspection

An unusual feature of this inspection was that the registered inspector was himself an English inspector and had been prominent nationally in English teaching matters through his involvement in the National Association for the Teaching of English (NATE). Don Meadows is also a member of NATE and, although knowing that the registered inspector was not going to be inspecting English, he was 'pleased that it was someone who had been involved in that organisation, which I have a lot of time for'. Don himself had hoped that the LEA inspectorate would win the inspection contract, not because he expected 'an easier ride' but because 'I know a fair number of them and I've worked with them and it would just have been more comforting to have faces that you knew and that you had already set up some sort of working relationship with'. However, he recognised that, if his LEA's team had won the contract, 'I have to say that the working relationships that had been set up in the past may have been severely strained that week.'

Headteacher Roy Adler had no prior knowledge of the inspection team, which was an independent team working through one of the major inspection agencies, although one of his deputies, who had previously worked as an LEA adviser, knew of some members and briefed him:

I then put out my feelers about the registered inspector and found that he was well respected in subject advisory work. And also, of course, I met a fellow head teacher whose school had been inspected by some of the team previously. There's so much time being spent on inspections and the word about registered inspectors gets around. Because the registered inspector is crucial to the inspection.

He was not concerned that the inspection was to be carried out by an independent team because he hadn't 'become enamoured' of the LEA he was now working in and in fact was very critical of it.

Janet Woolf had worked with some of the inspection team before but not with the registered inspector. Unlike some other inspectors, she had found the OFSTED training week to be 'excellent' because of the way it was 'organised to take us through the *Framework*' and, even though she found that 'the pressure was phenomenal', she liked 'writing to tight deadlines' but at the end felt 'relief that it was all over'. She has a very positive view about the OFSTED intention of 'improvement through inspection':

> The *Framework* is so well designed that, if we adhere to it, schools really should improve. It was all engineered by HMI, so many of them exceptionally talented, but what happens when that breed, with its academic rigour, has been eased out of the system?

Unlike some other schools in the case studies in this book, Sheriff High School did not take considerable steps to prepare itself for the OFSTED inspection. An inspector from the LEA was invited in to give a talk to the whole staff on the OFSTED procedures and processes for one hour during a staff training day some two terms beforehand. In addition, a staff training day at the start of the inspection term was given over to departments to use for their own preparations. Roy Adler recalls that:

> We were trying to concentrate on the school development plan and its implementation but as the autumn term went on there was an inevitable OFSTED twist to all meetings.

He also felt that the documentation requirements, particularly the headteacher form, put 'heavy demands on the school' and 'it was time I really could ill afford'. Even so, he emphasised that much of the paperwork was 'revisions of current papers' and he was at pains to stress that 'there was no big tart-up'.

Don Meadows meets regularly with a group of fellow heads of English from his part of the LEA and 'we talked quite a bit about OFSTED and the possibility of it – we had talked about the prospects of it'. At another meeting for all heads of English in the LEA, 'one head of department said that it hadn't been as bad as she'd expected, so that was fairly reassuring'. Both he and Angela felt that the talk by the LEA inspector had been helpful because 'it gave us some idea of what to expect – the sort of procedures, what was happening on different days, who was going to be looking at different departments'.

Don Meadows himself had a clear attitude to the whole inspection:

> Right from the start my aim had been to keep the emotional temperature of the department down, because I feel that all teachers, myself included, tend to be very self-critical and we need to value ourselves more. Because otherwise you can undermine everything you do. That was one of my aims. So, when I panicked, I got on the phone to another head of English I know.

So he constantly sought to reassure teachers in his department that they were 'doing a good job' and 'tried to keep the paperwork down to a minimum', so they didn't create materials that were not in existence before because 'I assumed the inspectors would have spotted that a mile off if we had'. He tried to check the departmental handbook, which had been updated on the arrival of Roy Adler as headteacher in the previous year, against the *Framework*:

> But I found it all a bit too much actually. Things that I simply couldn't work out or that I didn't have time for... we hoped it would just fit. It was a working document and we had deliberately set out not to put in there things we didn't do, so that it was of some use to us.

Angela Smith has little recall of what internal preparations the department undertook, which is perhaps indicative of the skilful manner in which Don Meadows managed the situation:

> I can't think. I can't honestly remember. We purposely didn't put on a show. We did prepare things as we would normally. We didn't have to do very much new at all, because we only had to produce schemes of work and I think Don would have had it all to hand. It's quite a good department in that way. We try to do things for each other rather than not communicating and keeping your ideas to yourself.

Going into the inspection, Angela was worried about 'who was going to be in the classroom and whether I'd behave any differently because they were there'. She was also anxious that she didn't disturb the relationships with her pupils by acting differently during the inspection.

Don Meadows's concerns were greater:

> Personally, what I felt was, because you don't know how it will turn out, I just knew I would be really gutted if at the end of the week someone had turned round and said it was awful, you just need to start from scratch. Because, I mean, I don't go round telling lots of people but I know how much time I spend on school work at home. So if that had happened, that was my nightmare scenario. And also, if it had been something fundamental, if it was just that everything I'd thought about and the way I managed things was wrong, then I knew that I couldn't change myself. That was the way I was

going to do things and I couldn't alter that fundamentally. The other slight problem, though I didn't worry about this too much, was that, because there are many things which have happened to English teaching recently that I am absolutely opposed to, I suppose I was slightly concerned that in would come people who'd say 'You've got to believe in that – put all those thoughts aside'.

During the inspection

From her reading of the materials sent to her before the inspection, Janet Woolf had formed the impression of an English department that was 'pretty successful and probably more imaginative than the rest of the school', although she was concerned about the overall reading standards throughout the school and about the fact that it seemed as if 'too many explanations were given for mediocre results overall, but not in English'. Arriving at the school she felt 'the usual slight tension at being amongst strangers' and went through 'the usual double-checking that I had all the necessary documentation in order'. Don Meadows was 'really nervous that morning' while Angela Smith 'wondered how many lessons they would be in'. Headteacher Roy Adler recalls driving to school that Monday morning:

> I hoped I wouldn't be late. This is it. We're as ready as we can be. And let's get on with it. I won't say I was looking forward to it but, when you've got ready for something and you've been waiting a long time for it, you just want to get on with it.

From his conversations with teaching staff during that day, he felt that the questions most people were asking were of the 'Was it OK?' and 'Did you get any feedback?' variety. There was a considerable sense of relief, he felt, 'that inspectors had the right number of heads'. Angela Smith recalls that most of her colleagues were apprehensive until they had had their first classroom observation. Don Meadows remembers that everyone was 'hypersensitive' but also that some of his fellow teachers were reporting friendly approaches by inspectors.

Don's first meeting with Janet Woolf was at a lunchtime computer club, at which he felt 'a bit awkward' because he wasn't quite sure 'how much we were talking on the record or off the record' to someone who was 'for that week an important person'. He would have preferred a more formal planned meeting as the first contact with the inspector, particularly because he was hearing about the English inspector visiting lessons 'before I'd even set eyes on her'. Janet Woolf remembers thinking that:

This was a sensitive, creative, hard-working person feeling understandable tension at the prospect of the week ahead but also one who was proud of much of the department's work.

However, she picked up from her own observations and from informal conversations with fellow inspectors that Sheriff High was a 'prickly school, on the defensive more than is usual in inspections'.

Don Meadows also remembers that other departments were reporting 'very chatty and friendly approaches' which the English department didn't feel they had at that point. However, on reflection now he sees that 'maybe by the end of the week you don't feel any better for the friendly approach'. As the week progressed, this became a noticeable issue for Roy Adler too:

> Whether the subject inspectors were being fair, that was the main concern. And in effect the different treatment of the subjects by inspectors, the different styles they adopted.

Headteacher Roy Adler had asked teachers to keep a record of the time spent by individual inspectors in subject lessons 'so that we would know, if a judgement was made, how many lessons had been seen in that subject in a particular year group – to check the evidence base'. He had also, quite properly, asked staff to inform him of any concerns arising during the week so that he could raise such matters with the registered inspector. One such issue arose in the inspection of English. Don Meadows described it thus:

> It was a teacher who only taught one group for English, so she was a little less confident but, having said that, I knew how much effort she put into English and I wanted to support her. What had happened was that she was in the middle of teaching when she was asked questions, with the group there and pupils overhearing the questions, and that had thrown her. She was doing something on the board with the class, which they were discussing, and her perception was that the lesson was going really well.

Janet Woolf recalls the incident somewhat differently:

> I asked for lesson notes and was told they were not available. I asked if perhaps they could be available on the following day and was told they couldn't. The teacher complained to the head of department. The head and the registered inspector talked this over and the registered inspector told me about the concern.

Such a minor incident serves to demonstrate the tensions that can exist during an inspection week. Janet Woolf subsequently sought out Don Meadows to apologise for the misunderstanding and the incident was quickly forgotten, although Don recalls that 'there was a bit of a hurt atmosphere' for the rest of that day.

In general, however, relationships between all concerned were maintained satisfactorily throughout the inspection. Angela Smith said that 'we had made a decision to act normally, the whole department' and, despite her apprehensions, she felt that she had behaved normally in lessons where she was observed and she found Janet Woolf's comments 'not too bad – she made some good comments and some fair criticisms as well'. Janet recalls feeling pleasure during lesson observations, 'wanting to join in and stopping myself' in several good lessons and 'longing to do it myself' in less satisfactory ones. She was impressed with the 'wide range of successful strategies, some very imaginative' used by Don Meadows and several of his colleagues and remembers vividly 'a sixth-form lesson on American literature in which media techniques were used' which she felt was outstanding.

The subsequent inspection report on the school identified the 'warm and friendly relationships between staff and pupils' for praise and Roy Adler felt that, during the inspection week, pupils had conducted themselves 'in a positive way to the school, they tried to support the school', a view shared by Don Meadows. Angela Smith felt pupils' reactions were varied:

> Some classes played up because there was somebody in. Others were a lot better perhaps than normal but generally those that I had were more or less the same as ever.

So, as the week was drawing to its close, Janet Woolf was thinking about giving her oral feedback to Don Meadows:

> I wanted to tell the truth as I saw it about this department which had so many good features and which could be even better. I didn't want to hurt any feelings. I was glad that I could say such praising things but anxious that what I said would be based on firm evidence which I could produce if challenged.

Don Meadows knew by now that his 'nightmare scenario' was not going to happen and he felt fairly comfortable because Janet had said 'a number of pleasant things and obviously some concerns' already to him. However, he does remember:

> This is me being petty really but I did worry a bit because, having moaned, I thought I might get my come-uppance when this report was written. I didn't think she'd do that really. It was all a bit of a build-up again. I was worried about it on the Friday morning. I think it was the set-up, though, I don't think it was Janet at all. You know, it's this going up to the deputy head's room and the deputy head will be there writing it down. It's almost like taking your solicitor along with you, it's that style.

Janet Woolf remembers that Don 'looked nervous at the start' of the oral feedback and she felt 'real sympathy for him' and was glad that the deputy headteacher 'seemed so pleased with a lot of what I said'. She was also 'anxious about speaking too quickly', which she recognises as a character trait of hers. She was conscious of the guidance given during her OFSTED training week that what is said in the feedback should come as no surprise to the recipient if the inspector has done his or her job properly through the week, 'I thought consciously during this feedback that the talks we had had through the week had prepared the way.'

Don Meadows recalls feeling at first relieved and then 'a lot of pleasure because there were lots of nice things said about the department and also that it was fair because the aspects that are weaker I agreed with'. As he left the deputy head's room, his first thoughts were to tell the rest of the department that it had been a good report but also he was 'conscious that there could be other people who weren't so happy and you've got to think about those other people':

> That's not because I want to make myself out to be some kind of saintly person but I knew how I'd have felt, because I'd gone through this scenario many times. If there had been lots of criticism, I'd have felt really awful about it. So I was really pleased but tried to keep it low-key.

He was particularly anxious about one of his colleagues whose department was criticised because he 'happened to know that this person was liable to depressions' and he was concerned for this colleague because 'it does matter a lot to people, doesn't it?'

After the inspection

At the end of the week, made more difficult by heavy snowfalls on the Tuesday and Wednesday which had had an inevitable impact on travelling conditions, all concerned were relieved that it was over. Janet Woolf recalls being 'glad to get out of that dark and poky room in which we had to work – I hated it' but also 'a belief that I had done the job as well as I could – there were no second thoughts about my judgements'. Don Meadows too felt relieved but also there was 'a boost because it had been good'. Angela Smith too was relieved 'even if it was better and less hassle than you'd expected it to be'.

When the final report on Sheriff High School was published, headteacher Roy Adler noted that:

> The written report was the same as the draft report. All the general bits, because they had been discussed so thoroughly beforehand and we had

verbatim transcripts of what had been said, had no surprises. We thought they were fair. Where we had real concerns were with the subject reports, when the oral feedback had included lots of positive things which were not in many cases reflected in the report. And that showed the skill of the inspectors in that teachers received the positive oral feedback whereas the written reports were sometimes received with horror.

The English department had no such problems, however. In the midst of what is a generally very positive report written by Janet Woolf, there are comments such as 'Much of the pupils' written work is lively and imaginative', 'Pupils speak enthusiastically in oral work', 'Discussion at sixth-form level is often of an impressive standard', and 'Some very good teaching takes place within the department'. With particular reference to Don Meadows himself, the report states:

> The department is very well managed. Excellent guidance is given to teachers through schemes of work, in-service training, collaborative discussion and the effective deployment and sharing of resources.

Don Meadows felt that all of this fitted with the oral feedback, though Angela Smith felt 'disappointed with the tiny amount of comment' in the written report – a feeling echoed by many teachers and inspectors.

Subsequent to the inspection and arising from issues identified in it, the department has been working on differentiated schemes of work related to particular class readers in order to find different tasks for different pupils 'to help with the range of ability'. Don Meadows produced a new assessment scheme in line with Janet Woolf's suggestions but, as Angela pointed out, 'Now the orders for National Curriculum English are changing anyway, that was a waste of time.' Another issue identified, though as a whole-school issue, was the need to improve reading standards at Key Stage 3. Angela again noted that, 'It's brought the attention of the other subjects and what they can do to help'. Both she and Don mentioned that a paired reading scheme involving pupils in Years 8 and 10 was being started. Don Meadows was also involved in work with the school's main feeder primary schools to help them to develop reading policies.

Being a local resident, Don was also aware of some local reaction to the school's inspection report. 'The press reaction was ecstatic,' he recalls, 'which was very good publicity for the school', although he had noticed that another local school which had been inspected subsequently had received similar headlines from the local press. Altogether though, he felt, 'the report will have boosted parental confidence in the school'.

Final perceptions

Janet Woolf – English inspector
The OFSTED inspection is a good first stage. Its value would be increased if there were a visit by the registered inspector a year later to see what had been done in the light of the report. I enjoyed seeing several inspectors I had worked with previously and meeting new ones, although one of the human difficulties of OFSTED is that one cannot experience the team cohesion of often working with the same team.

Angela Smith – second in English department
It probably focused us a bit more on the things that we'd been talking about so that we started doing things about them rather than just talking. I think the stress on the reading was a good thing. I don't think it's totally happened yet but it's one of the things on the Action Plan. They also mentioned using the library more for research in the different subjects. I think it was effective because some good things were pointed out. You know yourself the good things but you don't see them splashed over the newspapers, I mean good lessons and such. You tend to see sports and things like that. But the inspection cost a lot of money.

Roy Adler – headteacher
Yes it's been of some value. Not worth the money, however. In that I think it's taken us forward one term but backwards two terms, if you see what I mean. That's no criticism of the registered inspector or the team but rather of the process. It's a very heavy instrument – a very powerful one but still rather heavy. And, if it does continue, then the next time round, when it looks at what we have done in response, it may be more critical of our actions, it may be useful.

Don Meadows – head of English
In the end it gave us a boost. It's got rid of this thing that was looming. And they said we were okay, so we can go on and we've got that as a benchmark. So that, if our results in the summer are awful, we can say 'Well, they did look us over fairly thoroughly and there was nothing wrong with our teaching. It may be, therefore, that it's the exam that's wrong.' That could be useful for us. And it has been a personal help. I think I am fairly confident personally but there's a lot of me that isn't. I

was recently involved in preliminary interviews for a new deputy headteacher and they asked me what I felt about the inspection week and I had to say I didn't find it a pleasurable week, I found it very stressful and I was exhausted by the end of it. The eventual outcome was good for us and, as I said, that gave me a boost. But the actual week, not through any fault of the team concerned, is etched in my mind as horrendous really.

CHAPTER 6

A Beacon Light: Queen Mary's Grammar School for Girls (11–18)

Background

Queen Mary's Grammar School for Girls is situated in the heart of a northern city. Surrounded by extensive playing fields and bordered by parklands – 'Enormous trees soar upwards. Ducks settle on the pond. Squirrels dart about the woodland', as its brochure eloquently describes it – it has existed as a grammar school for girls for over 70 years. Until two years ago it had been an LEA school, with a long tradition of providing a high-quality academic education for the girls of the city, many of whom had gone on to prestigious universities and to success in the professions. In 1993, in order to preserve its grammar school status, it became grant-maintained.

Queen Mary's is a three-form entry school and admission to the school is by an 11+ examination. The majority of its pupils are recruited from the top 10 per cent of the ability range, as judged by this examination, and more than 90 per cent of them go on to higher education at the age of 18. There is a strong middle-class element in the pupil population, though the full socio-economic range is represented. The school is proud to reflect the full ethnic mix of its city and the pupil photographs chosen for its brochure reflect this mixture.

The academic prowess of the school is well demonstrated in its recent examination results, with 97 per cent of its pupils achieving five or more grades A–C at GCSE and with an 89 per cent pass rate at A level. These results place the school towards the top of the government's league tables, both in comparison with all schools and in comparison with other selective girls' schools nationally. The English department makes a significant contribution to these outstanding examination results, with all pupils achieving grades A–C at GCSE (50 per cent at grade A) and all pupils passing A level (33 per cent achieving grade A) in 1993. Over half of the pupils in the sixth form choose to study A level English literature. This, then, is a high-achieving department in a high-achieving school.

Joyce Sedgley had been appointed as headteacher of the school in the same year that it sought and was given grant-maintained status. In appointing her to the post, the governors had no doubt been anxious to ensure that she shared their views about the future direction of the school. In her previous 25 years of teaching, in both the state and independent sectors, she had experienced five short HMI inspections, always when she had been a head of department. She does not recall feeling 'particularly anxious' about any of these inspections at the time, being 'confident in the department's strengths, the motivation of the teachers and the success of the department' and therefore 'quite pleased to show outsiders what we could achieve'. However, she admits that she was 'unaware of the implications that the inspections had for anyone outside my area'.

> It didn't impinge on me that senior management might be having their own anxieties about the implications of the report. Of course, that's very useful for me now.

Kirsty Wigton, who had been head of English at Queen Mary's for eight years at the time of the OFSTED inspection after six years teaching in an independent school in the same city, had no experience of inspections to draw on. Neither did her colleague Audrey Wright who had only five years of teaching experience behind her and who was on maternity leave when the school first heard it was due for an inspection. Both, however, had recent experience of being appraised – in Kirsty's case by the deputy headteacher and in Audrey's case by the second in the English department. Both found these to be positive experiences, although they confessed to feeling nervous at the time.

Michael Peacock, who inspected the work of the English department at Queen Mary's, had been a headteacher in both the state and independent sectors for 17 years, after ten years as an English teacher and head of English. He decided to give up his headteacher post in order to 'branch out, partly into inspection work' as an educational consultant. With his wide experience of managing schools, he is in demand both nationally and internationally to offer consultancy on establishing and managing secondary schools. He recalls his OFSTED training week as being 'enjoyable, although I didn't find it terribly demanding' and found it to be a good introduction to the *Framework for Inspection*. His views about OFSTED's intention of 'improvement through inspection' are quite clear:

> I thought, and still think, that the clarity of the new process, and its invitation to schools to get themselves in order in whatever way best suits their approach to the *Framework*, is itself a valid, improving process. Given this, the inspection itself becomes a more accurate measure of the school's response, though I do regret the absence of post-inspection dialogue.

His only experience of inspection was when a school of which he was headteacher received a full inspection from its LEA inspectorate, an experience he found to be 'helpful, giving plenty of insights', although he admits that it was only during the course of the inspection that he became aware 'how stressful the process was for the staff and how much better it would have been with careful pre-inspection measures' by himself and the LEA.

Dramatis personae

Joyce Sedgley – headteacher (28 years teaching experience, including two years as headteacher).
Kirsty Wigton – head of English (14 years teaching experience, including eight years as head of English at Queen Mary's).
Audrey Wright – English teacher (five years teaching experience).
Michael Peacock – English inspector (27 years teaching experience, including 17 years as headteacher).

Before the inspection

Joyce Sedgley regretted the demise of Her Majesty's Inspectorate because she believed that HMI judgements were balanced and objective and that HMIs did not have a 'political agenda'.

> I didn't feel in any sense that the department or the school would be any the worse after their visit than before, whereas I was not sure that in the case of the OFSTED inspections that would be so. Because the OFSTED inspection came at a time when standards in schools were alleged to be falling and teachers obviously had a great responsibility for this. So it was the background in which the OFSTED inspections were announced which made me as a headteacher very anxious.

Kirsty Wigton felt that OFSTED inspections could be 'less

controllable, more variable in experience from team to team'. Although she had no prior experience of being inspected, she had been used to the supportive nature of the advice offered by the English inspector of the school's former LEA with whom she felt she worked 'side by side'. Her reaction on hearing that Queen Mary's was to be inspected was one of fear, although she felt even more sorry for a fellow head of English in a nearby comprehensive school whose school was to be inspected in the very first month of the new system:

> I remember feeling relieved that it was to be in the summer term, that it was put off that far, because we'd be able to get more prepared for it, in terms of finding out how the inspection went for other schools.

Audrey Wright, being at the time of the announcement of the impending inspection absent from the school on maternity leave, found that she 'didn't have the same amount of panic as everybody else had at the time'. She remembers that there was a sort of expectation among the staff that the school would be inspected at some time and she felt that this might be a good thing.

> I thought if a school like ours doesn't do well, it would reflect on OFSTED. I have to say, however, that I became increasingly horrified as the first wave went through and we started getting reports on the television of schools that had been failed. One of the primary schools that failed, a member of my family knows the school and she was very surprised that that had happened, because in her opinion the school didn't deserve the reputation it had been given. So my feelings about what OFSTED could do changed as a consequence.

Joyce Sedgley was concerned that the contract might go to the school's former LEA inspectorate after the school had recently left that LEA to become grant-maintained, not because she mistrusted the professional integrity of the members of that inspectorate but because she felt that the LEA was politically opposed to selective schools. She was also anxious because she herself was relatively new in the post of headteacher.

> So there was a lot of anxiety for me personally, because while you can say that you can't and have no wish to change everything in a very short time, you will be held accountable for the situation in the school, whether it's to do with you personally and your management as a head or whether it was to do with what went on under the LEA or whatever.

Although a part of her wanted an LEA team to conduct the inspection because 'it's my experience that they come with a very positive view of guiding schools to move further forward' Joyce Sedgley felt it was inevitable when the school was informed that an independent team of inspectors would be carrying out the inspection. She discovered that the registered inspector was a former HMI who had been a member of a team which had inspected a school she had previously worked in. Another member of the team was 'a former head of another selective school' in a neighbouring town, 'which might have been a potential difficulty – I knew of his reputation'.

Kirsty Wigton had 'no strong feelings about the team membership' when she heard about it.

Since it wasn't an LEA team, it was an independent group, I had no links or associations or expectations whatsoever. Completely blind really.

Michael Peacock's name meant nothing to her and 'the few people I asked didn't know of him', so she was unable to get any information about him before the inspection.

In fact, it was only at the very end of the inspection that I asked him what his background was and he apologised for not having told me to start with. So I asked him where he was from and what was his background and what was his past.

Audrey Wright had expected an independent team, but she had no knowledge of any of its members when the names were learnt. However, she was considerably reassured when the registered inspector and some of his colleagues visited the school in advance and spoke to the staff about their philosophy of 'working within the OFSTED *Framework* but trying to be positive'.

In preparation for the inspection, the school allocated a training day when two registered inspectors from a neighbouring LEA, bought in by Queen Mary's, took the whole staff through the processes of the inspection as outlined in the *Framework for Inspection*. Audrey Wright was particularly reassured by a video of an English lesson which she watched with colleagues from other subject areas, although it received 'a very mixed reaction' from some of those colleagues. In addition, Joyce Sedgley and her senior management team directed in-service provision towards areas of the school. This in-service provision was bought in from a number of neighbouring LEAs where she had been told 'that the advice was compatible with our expectations or was sympathetic to our approach'. So, the school did not buy in a total pre-inspection package, but shopped around for where they believed they could get the best guidance in a particular subject or area. This guidance was largely directed towards subject areas, but the 'senior management team also had some in-service to prepare them and there was quite a lot of preparation for governors as well'. Overall, Joyce felt that the money was well spent.

As their part of this preparation, the English inspector from one of the neighbouring LEAs spent a day in the school inspecting the English department. Kirsty Wigton recalls:

> I think it helped because it was a positive thing. The fear builds up in advance
> of OFSTED and the external support that we had reassured us that inspectors
> were human beings and the kind of people we had been working with all the
> time. He said very positive and encouraging and supportive things. He gave
> feedback on lessons he had observed in OFSTED terminology. And that was
> helpful.

Audrey Wright also felt this visit to be 'very reassuring', because 'he
gave us an honest opinion and then he gave us an OFSTED version of it'.

On her appointment to the school, Joyce Sedgley remembers being
impressed at 'how well-progressed departmental handbooks were'.
Nevertheless, she was sure that 'the impression that is made on the
inspection team starts as soon as they receive the schemes of work', so
further secretarial help was engaged to ensure that all of the departmental
handbooks were even more 'professionally produced' and followed 'a
similar format'. However, because the school had been involved in 'a
massive undertaking to re-present policies to governors as a grant-
maintained school', a large amount of the school's documentation was in
good order and very little new writing was necessary.

> There were no new systems set up. We were very wary of doing that because
> we did not want to cause any cynicism amongst our head of department
> colleagues. We made no bones about the fact that, when the inspection team
> came, we would sell ourselves for all we were worth because that's what an
> inspection is about. And if you couldn't put on good lessons in your
> inspection when could you? We were quite up-front about that, quite ruthless
> about that. But there were no new systems.

In re-organising the English department handbook, Kirsty Wigton
asked each member of her team to take responsibility for a particular year
group in order to upgrade the previous schemes of work and ensure that
a more specific list of National Curriculum-related activities was
included. However, as Audrey Wright remembers:

> What we had before was much more of an outline scheme of work. What we
> did was to look at what we had been doing in classes over the past couple of
> years. We looked initially at what had worked. We stuck as much as possible
> to our original ideas but we had a more structured list of activities that would
> feed directly into the programmes of study.

Michael Peacock's first view of the English department was, naturally,
through this handbook, which impressed him:

> It was a model of clarity and thoroughness. This, with the outstanding
> examination results in English, suggested a very competent, professional

department.

The inspection was timed for the second week of the summer term and the time immediately before was a time of considerable stress for the English department. Audrey Wright 'had virtually no Easter holiday – I even sent my daughter to the childminder for a week' so that she could prepare work carefully and ensure that all marking was up to date. 'You felt that if things were not looking as though they were absolutely ship-shape, it would be you letting the side down.'

Kirsty Wigton, who also sent her children to a childminder for part of the Easter holidays, also had concerns going into the inspection:

I know I've got a good department. We get good results and we're a popular department. We get lots of girls who want to do English at A level. The atmosphere is nice and the girls enjoy their lessons. My anxiety was that this wouldn't come over. I wanted to be judged the way we really are. It's the pressure of having to do it all in the one week I think. We had to prove we did what we did well during that week.

She also called a departmental meeting towards the end of the previous term to review everyone's intentions during the week in order to ensure the 'representativeness' of the work of the department. Some difficult decisions were made at that meeting:

For instance, we have a reading period once a week with Year 7 and Year 8. At one stage the temptation was not to do that. Because why does an inspector want to come in and see 32 girls reading and one girl talking to a member of staff? But we decided we would keep that in.

Joyce Sedgley's main concerns going into the inspection were less, because she felt that the 'anxieties were earlier on' for her, but largely it was 'the housekeeping details that concerned me' – 'Actually on Sunday morning I came in and I went round the school and I tidied it!'

During the inspection

Audrey Wright arrived at school on the Monday morning of the inspection week 'panic-stricken because I needed to get on the photocopier for something I desperately needed that morning and I couldn't! I got in a real flap about it'. This was a reference in a scheme of work specifically for grammar and punctuation 'which I do normally in preparation for or following from a piece of written work', but which she felt she had to foreground more clearly within the written scheme of work and had spent the Sunday evening writing up.

I began to calm down when I realised there wasn't an inspector sitting in my registration waiting for me. And when I got down to assembly and saw other people's faces, I began to calm down then.

Kirsty Wigton at the same time on the Monday was feeling 'absolutely relieved because all these things we had been preparing for the best part of a year I could actually start telling somebody, start showing somebody, actually start unburdening' – 'I felt as well prepared as we could ever be. Very nervous but well prepared.' Joyce Sedgley, arriving early at the school, felt 'quite calm'. The school had made careful preparations and she found that her major task with the inspectors arriving for the first time in Queen Mary's was in reiterating directions to various parts of the buildings.

Michael Peacock's initial perception on arriving at Queen Mary's was that 'everything was well organised for the week – the school was about its able and economical business as usual, and there'd be no sense of flap here'. By prior arrangement, he met with Kirsty Wigton soon after arriving and formed an impression of 'an intelligent, humane, highly professional person, well in command of her subject and department'. He also sensed very quickly that 'it would be possible to meet as colleagues and share ideas and perceptions as the inspection developed'. Kirsty recalls that Michael immediately made some very positive comments about the documentation and the examination results:

> He was trying to show that he was open-minded and batting for us, I think. Willing to look for good things as it were. Which I appreciated. That was good.

She found him friendly and open. Although she was curious about who he was and where he came from, she didn't feel it was appropriate to ask at this time. Kirsty took Michael Peacock into the departmental office at this stage to introduce him briefly to the rest of the department. Audrey Wright remembers forming the impression of someone 'quiet, unassuming, with a very gentle manner and very smiling – it didn't feel intimidating'.

Michael observed Kirsty's first lesson, a drama lesson with Year 8 – 'head of department's privilege, I suppose'. She felt the lesson went well and was pleased that Michael Peacock was positive and reassuring.

> He avoided OFSTED-speak at the end of lessons. He said things like 'They enjoyed that.' It wasn't in terms of what would be in the report, which was fair enough. I wasn't expecting to get fours and threes and twos for quality of learning or whatever.

Audrey Wright's first lesson observation came later that morning.

When Michael entered the classroom, she felt her 'heart miss a beat', but then she relaxed because she 'was in full flow, beginning to talk through the process of what the girls were going to do' in a poetry-writing lesson. She also appreciated the feedback he gave at the end of the lesson about having enjoyed what had been seen and having found the lesson very constructive: 'He was always very positive about the girls. He was always prepared to talk about what he had observed, to some degree'.

As far as the English department was concerned, then, prior apprehensions were rapidly softened by the approach taken by Michael Peacock. Conversation in the staffroom that Monday confirmed that, compared with the experience in some other subjects, the English inspector was 'a good one, someone who was interested and knew his stuff, someone who was fairly positive'. Michael Peacock's own early perceptions echoed this:

> Early in the week I began to get comments and notes. The impression gained from other departments was that the English department was highly regarded within the school. Standards of written presentation were high, as was the level of discussion and debate. Clearly, the pupils were using their English skills to good effect in other lessons.

As the week progressed, members of the Queen Mary's English department became calmer and more confident in their work. Audrey Wright was observed teaching on six occasions and felt generally satisfied with the way her lessons went, though one Year 7 class went less well than it might have done and she felt her planning for that lesson could have been better. Kirsty Wigton was 'very aware that he was in the corner of the room the whole time – I couldn't forget that, at any point' during classroom observations and was happier when she was in 'non-didactic modes, in small group work'. She felt that the girls at times were also uncomfortable, particularly a lower-sixth group:

> They had prepared a presentation on an A level topic essay and then normally there would have been questions from the students to the three on the panel who had done the presentation. And I sort of led them into questions and nothing came. I tried a few more tacks and approaches and still nothing came! They were all sitting there startled. Perhaps they found it harder than the juniors.

In another lesson, however, with a Year 10 group taught by Audrey Wright when the class were at work with computers, Michael Peacock commented that the girls hadn't done much. One girl, overhearing this, asked Audrey if she could show him her folder of all their IT work done previously. Kirsty felt that staff in general did not take as many gambles in their teaching and that they 'probably didn't do any new work' but she cited examples of how members of the department used ideas developed by others for the first time during that week.

Kirsty did feel that she worked no harder in the inspection week than normally, but the emphasis of her work changed – 'I did no marking that week'. Audrey Wright felt 'everybody was in overdrive' and she herself 'only had five hours sleep a night' and that it was a much more demanding week than any she had experienced previously in her teaching career, 'If this is what we're supposed to be doing normally, then how would we cope?'

Michael Peacock continued to be impressed by the English department and its work. He noted that 'lessons were very competently organised', that Kirsty Wigton was 'very generous with time, which enabled me to refine my views and ask new questions', and that 'teachers were keen to draw both the literary and IT prowess of the department to my attention and I was impressed with both':

> There was no apparent change in diet for the week, and teachers were willing to show me the whole process – planning, teaching, assessing, recording – for any given class.

So, as the week drew to a close, the English department awaited the formal report from Michael Peacock in a very optimistic manner. Audrey Wright and her colleagues 'expected it to be quite good' because they 'knew they had lots of things going for them in terms of results', none of them had had lessons that went other than well, and they had also received a very positive report from the LEA English inspector who had conducted their brief pre-inspection. There had also been a number of 'snippets of information' that the department was highly regarded for certain developments such as in differentiation.

Kirsty Wigton also referred to some of these 'snippets' that had 'come through other channels' and she mentioned that, on the day after the inspectors had looked at the representative sample of work from every year group:

> Word had come back that we had come out of that very well, both in terms of our assessment procedures and the marking procedures that we use and in terms of the interviews with the girls, who were very positive about our policies. An expression was used of us that we were a 'beacon light' within the school. That was good!

So she was hoping for a good report.

Michael Peacock in preparing his report 'wanted to pay an objective tribute to the quality of the department and its results, as well as making a full, professional evaluation', although he was aware of how difficult this was in such a short period of time.

Kirsty Wigton felt 'terrified' going into the feedback session 'partly because of the formality of it – it wasn't just him and me, there were four of us in a little room and it was hot'. Even though she was aware that Michael was giving positive signs through smiling and through his body language, she found the experience nerve-racking. In terms of what was said:

It was positive but I heard the 'satisfactories'. The 'goods' and the 'very goods' are there, when you look at the written report. But the 'satisfactory' is what hits you first, the fact that all lessons were satisfactory and 78 per cent were good or very good. It's that 'satisfactory' when you feel that you're doing a lot more than just being satisfactory. So I was actually disappointed at the end of that because of the 'satisfactory'.

Kirsty's disappointment was added to by the discovery that some of her fellow heads of department were feeling much more elated after their feedbacks because words like 'excellent' and 'outstanding' had been used. This made her even more deflated at that stage 'especially when everything had been suggesting that it would be positive – the beacon light idea and so on':

In retrospect and once the report had been published, I think he was very fair because what he did in the feedback was read out what he had written and so I got the deflation at that point and other colleagues got it from the written report because the 'excellents' don't appear in the written reports.

At that point, Kirsty felt that she had not received the report she expected, probably because, as she acknowledged, the stresses of the week were forcing her to take an unbalanced view of what was said.

Michael Peacock was not aware of Kirsty's feelings. In giving his oral feedback, he thought that 'feelings all round were pretty good':

The department was a model – well-run, good results, excellent assessment and recording procedures, good resources. It was more a question of validating what they did and encouraging good practice. I felt that I had managed to do justice to the department and the OFSTED framework.

This mismatch between the inspector's perception of the oral feedback and the head of department's is one seen in other case studies and deserves further attention.

After the inspection

At the end of the inspection week, all concerned at Queen Mary's felt drained and glad that it was all over. Kirsty Wigton, having talked through with her department the full report she had received from the copious notes she had taken during the oral feedback session, realised that her disappointment was an over-reaction and that, even though she had not received the glowing report she might have wanted, nevertheless her department had been highly praised by Michael Peacock for its good work. The department, which works closely as a team, was brought more closely together by the experience and supported each other throughout the week, 'They are a wonderful team. We came through the experience together. It's a strong team that was made even stronger.'

Joyce Sedgley and her two deputies had attended all the subject feedbacks, even though there were some organisational problems in arranging for these feedbacks because the registered inspector was not able to give details of these until the first morning of the inspection week. Having had a presence at all of these feedbacks, she knew that the inspection was going to prove positive. However, she was rather cautious:

> It depends on the nature of your personality. I wish I were more aggressive and assertive. I tend to be rather introspective and rather questioning and I'm always looking for the snags. I misread it all completely. I misread it as a rather cool view of the school. In fact it's a very positive view of the school. But I think that's to do with my personality.

She had been aware that Kirsty Wigton, who she regarded as a 'quite outstanding head of department', had been disappointed by her feedback and she was concerned that there was 'some imbalance in the reporting'. Some of this unevenness she put down to the fact that subject inspectors 'come with their own agenda' and don't see the overall school picture.

She had also received an oral report from the registered inspector and his deputy, when she was not allowed to have her deputies present. She found that 'very difficult' because 'all I could see were the negatives and that caused me a great deal of anxiety. I think I had the most unpleasant weekend of my life afterwards'. She subsequently presented the registered inspector with some supplementary evidence which helped to modify the perceptions which led to one of the main comments made.

When the registered inspector returned one week later to read the draft report, Joyce Sedgley felt much more positive about what she was hearing, although she was aware that she was still listening for criticisms 'to see how they will be interpreted by the parents and by the press'. By the time the final written report was published, she realised that it was a very good one, referring to the high standards of teaching and of achievement in the school:

> Even the most mischievous press would have a job to do anything really wicked with it. Because the things that matter most to our parents – quite reasonably in a selective school – are that the teaching standards are high,

lessons are intellectually stimulating, and results are higher than similar schools nationally.

The published report on English includes the following:

The quality of pupils' learning was satisfactory or better in all lessons observed, good or very good in over three-quarters. Pupils enjoy the subject, make considerable gains in skills, knowledge and understanding and work well together. Pupils discuss a range of issues, show a good command of vocabulary and argument and reach critical judgements on some demanding texts. Pupils read with skill and enjoyment, often at a mature level. They make good use of silent reading time and of the book boxes which were available in class. Pupils write with clarity, accuracy and cogency in a variety of genres, responding well to the often demanding tasks they are given. The quality of handwriting, spelling, grammar and punctuation is good and pupils show evidence of careful drafting and redrafting.

Kirsty Wigton, on reading the published report, was quite happy with it, although she still felt that alongside the reports on other departments:

There is still the unevenness in the way things are described. We don't have quality of teaching, quality of learning for every department. It should be consistent, I think. One way or the other.

Audrey Wright was also concerned about this perceived unevenness. She was surprised to see the word 'excellent' used elsewhere when they had been told that 'very good' would be the highest term used.

Subsequent to the publication of the report, Joyce Sedgley offered to let parents have a copy of the full report at a small charge, as well as the summary report, and over 100 parents took up this offer. The school also held an open meeting for parents, which was not particularly well attended but allowed parents to ask for clarification about particular matters. Since then, with the support of an *ad hoc* committee of governors, the school has put together its Action Plan which has been widely circulated in draft form, although Joyce Sedgley feels that the required time scale had made it very difficult to involve all staff in this plan's creation.

Final perceptions

Michael Peacock – English inspector
I think the English inspection was a positive affair. I'd be surprised if staff found it a negative experience, but could well accept that they found it a bit lacking in 'practical criticism' – partly because an inspection isn't about ideas, and partly because its main function was

to validate some very good practice. For the school, it should prove a useful validation of progress at this point in a new regime, which must encourage it to go forward with confidence and a touch more relaxation.

Joyce Sedgley – headteacher
If the heads of departments feel pleased and motivated through the inspection, then it was worth it. But I find it's an interruption to the serious work that has to be done in the school. And I feel confident that we would have tackled the issues that were raised, perhaps not in that order but we would have tackled them. I think it's unnecessary, a dreadful waste of resources. And I do think there are parents who will still feel cynical about our very good report. They will say it's bound to be good because it's a selective school. And there will always be parents who will question a report that says, shall we say, English is a beacon of light, they will still come and complain about standards of English somewhere in the school.

Audrey Wright – English teacher
There has to be some sort of regulatory process, checking that we are doing what we're supposed to do. Whether it has to be done this way is open to question. I got the impression that there are certain buzz-words and topics of the moment, like differentiation, and there seems to be a lot of focus on that. I was also anxious about inspectors jumping to conclusions. I wondered what sort of preconceptions they were actually coming into the school with. I think because we had a good report and we felt the judgements on the whole were very fair, my reactions were more positive than if we'd had a negative response. I suppose it is nice to have someone come in and say you are doing things OK.

Kirsty Wigton – head of English
I don't think it has had much value really. It's taken a lot of focus this year. In some respects on a whole-school basis it's made things easier but not in all. One thing that was nice in inspection week was that we kept the staffroom as an inspector-free area and it was the only part of the school that was, which meant that we had the senior management team in there as well, letting their hair down a little at times. And that was good because ordinary staff and senior management, because of the pressure of other things, don't always mix very much in school. That greater interaction was good. It hasn't carried on since then but...It's focused whole-school issues more. It's maybe clarified

certain points of department thinking more, such as the continuity and progression patterns. But I think it's very difficult to get a picture that's accurate in just one week like that. It's just one week at random and, unless you're going to manipulate your timetable, you're only going to get a picture and whether it's a representative picture, who knows? And there should be consistency, one way or the other. And more of a developmental aim would make it more beneficial to schools.

CHAPTER 7

Wriggleoutof: Axminster Modern School (12–16)

Background

Axminster Modern School is situated in a rural town in the south of England and serves an area covering approximately 120 square miles, stretching from the town to the surrounding parts of the county. The town itself, once an ancient market town but one which largely escaped the inroads of the industrial revolution, is within relatively easy driving distance of larger towns, which have higher concentrations of commercial and industrial businesses. In recent years it has witnessed a growth of modern commercial developments, which are less labour intensive and more reliant on state-of-the-art modern technology. The school's intake is drawn, according to census returns, from a population which is largely middle class and in full-time employment. Unemployment figures are below county and national averages.

The school takes pupils aged between 12 and 16 years and currently has about 900 pupils drawn from up to 17 contributory middle schools. Although it loses up to 25 per cent of its potential pupils to nearby selective schools, a relatively high proportion of its pupils is of average ability. There are only three pupils with statements of special educational need and a very small number of pupils from ethnic minority backgrounds. GCSE examination results are above average for similar schools nationally and in English are on a par with the national average for all schools. Well over half of the school's pupils transfer into full-time post-16 education.

Barbara Wynne had been headteacher at Axminster Modern School for six years prior to the OFSTED inspection. In that time she had overseen the merger of Axminster with another, smaller, neighbouring school and had witnessed the controversy caused by the county LEA's proposals to abandon the middle-school system and revert to transfer of pupils at the age of 11. In her 26 years of teaching, she had never experienced an inspection of any sort in any of the schools she had worked in. Her first reactions to the creation of OFSTED were ones of 'anxiety', though she 'hoped the school would be inspected sooner rather than later'. It seemed, she felt, 'initially to be a very cumbersome process'. When the contract for the inspection of Axminster was awarded to a neighbouring LEA's inspectorate, she was quite satisfied:

> I was quite pleased it wasn't our LEA's inspectors because obviously we know them well – they're in and out all the time. I think it's good to have some agency from outside monitoring the school. I think it's fairer somehow.

Carol Fisher, head of English at Axminster, and Jill Walsh, her deputy, had both taught for nearly 30 years, the last 20 of which had been in their current roles within the English department. Neither teacher had any prior experience of inspections either by HMI or by their LEA, nor had either experience of being observed teaching as part of the appraisal process, since the school was not yet fully geared up for the latter. Carol Fisher's reaction to the announcement of the OFSTED system was typically forthright:

> I thought it was a jolly good thing that schools should be examined. But when I realised that they would be examining me as well, I wasn't quite so chuffed. Because I knew that however well prepared you think you are, things are going to go wrong and you're going to be found wanting in areas you didn't expect. And, therefore, I believed that they should spend their time looking at these non-achieving schools, instead of wasting public money coming to look at us. That's pretty arrogant but that's exactly how I felt.

Jill Walsh was quite happy about the English department being inspected because she was confident in their work and results. She was aware, however, that the English staff 'tended to work too much in isolation as individuals' and there was a need for greater collaboration, so that the sharing of ideas which occurred 'in passing' was more structured 'to be able to show somebody from outside the extent of what was being done'.

Despite her apparent confidence, Carol Fisher admitted that, when she discovered the timing of the inspection, she was 'appalled because we knew there wouldn't be many people who could give us advice, and because we'd got so much on with the new National Curriculum and with the new exams, of course, so whenever they had come wouldn't have been a very good time'.

Neither Carol Fisher nor Jill Walsh had any knowledge of the inspection team, though Jill had heard from teachers she knew that the team were considered 'very good'. Neither had heard of or come across Martin Bunyan, the English inspector.

Dramatis personae

Barbara Wynne – headteacher (26 years teaching experience, including six years as headteacher).
Carol Fisher – head of English (29 years teaching experience, 20 as head of English at Axminster Modern).
Jill Walsh – second in English department (30 years teaching, 21 as second in English at Axminster Modern).
Martin Bunyan – English inspector.

Before the inspection

In preparation for the OFSTED inspection, headteacher Barbara Wynne attended a conference held in the centre of a neighbouring town, which was led by former HMIs, and one of her deputies attended a half-day conference mounted by the Secondary Headteachers Association (SHA). These two events helped them to understand the OFSTED *Framework* and to prepare for the inspection itself. The SHA conference, in particular, was considered to be 'very valuable'. As a result of these conferences and with the information gathered from them, Barbara Wynne and her senior management team led a training day for all staff to take them through the OFSTED *Framework*. During this day, guidance was given to heads of departments about revising their departmental handbooks and producing them in a common format. The staff handbook was also re-organised.

The LEA's English inspector was invited to spend a day in the school to help the English department in its preparations and she spent that day visiting classrooms and observing lessons. Carol Fisher was impressed with the feedback she received from this visit in the discussion she had with the English inspector after school hours:

Frankly, I was amazed at how much she'd picked up in that day. I was most impressed frankly by her *nous*. She really had picked up virtually all our strengths and some of the weaknesses as well. She'd certainly got an extremely informed opinion of the department in one day.

The English inspector pointed out to Carol Fisher a number of areas for improvement. The first was regarding the throwing away of old and out-of-date stock which was cluttering up classrooms and storage space. The second was concerned with the schemes of work which the department used:

We had handwritten schemes of work for about 50 books but she said these weren't good enough. Like the books, some of them were 20 years old and teaching has moved on a bit. And she suggested that we started renewing the schemes of work. We're text-based here – all the grammar comes from the literature. Well, as soon as I'd actually started, I really got rather excited. So by the time the inspection arrived, we'd actually got about 30 schemes of work, beautifully typed. A young member of the department designed some covers on a computer with computer images, cardboard covers and ring binders. They do look enormously impressive. And the contents frankly are quite impressive too.

Jill Walsh too felt that this work was beneficial.

I think overall we are happy with what OFSTED has given us in that sense, that we do have now a much more methodical means of tying together all these different schemes and all the schemes are now more readily available.

The English department handbook was also revised and brought up to date, though Carol had concerns in describing teaching methodology:

Within the English department, we all teach in our own ways provided the exam results are there at the end. But our different ways are equally successful.

Jill Walsh remembers that the substance of the LEA English inspector's visit was concerned with 'the appearance of the department – for example, a lot of files were kept in Persil boxes' and with 'certain aspects of teamwork that she thought we could spend more time working at'.

As part of a regular review of pupils' learning, the senior management team at Axminster conduct their own audit of departments by scrutinising documentation, looking at pupils' books and observing teachers at work. In the event, not all departments received this audit before the inspection, although the English department, protests notwithstanding, did. Carol Fisher recalls this:

It was a stress. They told us in advance which lessons they were going to come into. They knew I had two Year 11 classes that were difficult and they didn't choose either of those. But at least one got used to having someone in one's class. We all had two senior staff in two different classes. And there was a formal, official feedback.

This pre-inspection classroom observation by the senior management team, although at the time it was found to be stressful and demanding, was something that the English department was later grateful for, since hardly any member of the department had any prior experience since student days of being observed teaching. As a result of the comments received from these visits, there was quite a bit of tidying up in classrooms and 'more children's work was put up on display'.

As the inspection drew closer, Barbara Wynne was concerned 'that the inspectors would see the school in its true light and that the children and staff would behave as normally as possible'. Consequently, she only announced the OFSTED visit to the pupils on the Thursday before the inspection week. She was also a little anxious about some members of staff who were '*anti* the inspection' and might give 'a negative impression' and so she asked all staff 'to think before they spoke because throwaway comments might give the inspectors the wrong impression'.

Carol Fisher was anxious because she was aware that many of the staff in her department, including herself, were not sleeping properly and that her own confident manner ('I was exuding confidence for their benefit') might have taken its toll on her. 'All the time I was wondering if they'll find out things we've no idea we're not doing. I couldn't think what they could be.'

Jill Walsh's anxieties were more to do with ensuring that pupils' work was representative:

> I was anxious that, when the children's work was seen, we would be able to demonstrate that everything had been covered. You don't always consciously do this when you're teaching. You haven't necessarily got the piece of work formally to present at the end of it. So it was quite an anxiety how to show somebody who wanted to see everything all aspects of chosen children's pieces of work. I felt this was a bit time-consuming and this detracted from what we do normally with the children.

During the inspection

Headteacher Barbara Wynne was relieved when the week of the actual inspection at last came round. On the Monday morning, she came into school 15 minutes earlier than usual:

> To make sure that everything I needed for the week was actually laid out so that, if I got held up, I could just pick up that pile and know that everything I

needed was in it. Because you never know what kind of emergencies might occur.

Carol Fisher had other reasons for feeling relieved on that Monday morning:

Well, of course I was going to the opera that day! I announced to the staff that I was going to *Rigoletto* – you could call it *Wriggleoutof* – and you can imagine what their reaction was. But it was a difficult thing because the two classes I was worried about I didn't have that day. Which meant that the chances of being inspected during those classes were raised and frankly I was very worried indeed that I might be judged on 29 years teaching by being seen with one of those challenging groups.

The visit to *Rigoletto* was part of a joint project with a neighbouring school in collaboration with the Royal Opera House, which had been arranged months beforehand. The project involved pupils from the two schools working with actors, singers and a composer from the Royal Opera House, attending a performance of *Rigoletto*, and then writing their own operas, some of which were subsequently selected for performance in the town hall.

The burden of the first day's inspection of English, then, fell on to Jill Walsh. She knew that she had a meeting with Martin Bunyan during the second period on the Monday morning and she felt quite calm about that but she had a surprise when he came to observe her first lesson:

So I met him before I actually talked with him. But that turned out to be great as well. Because he was so nice in the lesson, he was so responsive to the children, he enjoyed what the children were saying. His manner was so nice, he was full of smiles. And that was great for the meeting that followed. I felt I'd already met him and he knew a bit about the department already and he knew a bit about me. In fact he knew more than perhaps he expected to know because, as it happened fortuitously, in that lesson I had brought in some newspaper cuttings. Three children in that class had their photographs in the local paper. So I'd brought these in to chat with them and it was all because of work they'd done in English. We'd had a visiting author in the autumn and as a result of that we'd become involved in the Readathon and we'd raised over £2000. So he'd learned about aspects of the department not necessarily concerned with the National Curriculum or OFSTED.

By the time Carol Fisher returned from her visit to the opera that afternoon, it was too late to find members of her department at the school so she phoned all of her colleagues in the evening. The general reaction she discovered was positive. She found from Jill Walsh that Martin Bunyan had been impressed by the documentation and she formed the impression that 'what he wanted to do was check that all the things we said we were doing in the handbook we were doing'. One particular feature which she learned was successful was the insistence by senior management that all staff completed lesson outlines to give to inspectors when they came into classrooms:

> Doing those sheets was salutary and very useful. I'm glad I had it to do because it forced me to get prepared. I was only doing the things I would normally do but it crystallised one's mind for that week.

Naturally, when she was back in school during the rest of the week, Carol Fisher experienced a number of lesson observations, during which she felt 'generally comfortable'. One lesson she remembers particularly well, because Martin Bunyan came to observe one of her Year 11 classes:

> This was one of my triumphs! The lesson he came into started with lots of teasing and laughter – 'He's here, he's here!' and of course he wasn't here at all. And then, their faces! – I knew he was here because of their faces. So I carried on with what I was doing. We were doing travel brochures, the literature of travel brochures. And then, to my horror, the door opened and a boy from the same year said, 'Excuse me, could you come urgently to Mr So-and-so's class'. So I went. I usually wear high heels and I always leave the door open so that they can hear me coming back, which means that they behave by the time I'm here. It saves a lot of time and aggro. Well, when I got back, they were sitting in exactly the same place where I'd left them and were working furiously! So, at least he'd seen a tricky class showing quite a degree of responsibility towards their teacher.

Jill Walsh also had a number of her lessons observed.

> The first lesson I really enjoyed myself, because I was praising the children and they were really pleased with what had been happening. And Martin Bunyan was very much a part of it. It was so nice to see him enjoying the children's pleasure.

She recalls how Martin Bunyan looked at pupils' books and talked to pupils, and particularly how he made a lot of notes about the pupils' writing that was displayed on the classroom walls. Another lesson, with a Year 11 top set, she was less happy with:

> I was going to put them into groups immediately we began the lesson. And I was conscious that I couldn't do this, because he walked in right at the beginning. I thought this was going to be dreadful if he just saw the groups. Perhaps it was wrong, because that was the way I would have taught that lesson. I shouldn't have changed it. But I felt I needed to put him in the picture about what we were doing.

Consequently, she spent time recapping previous discussion and planning 'really for him to know' and the class were giving her odd looks. She also felt confused because 'he sat on the periphery' watching the groups and didn't get closer to any of the group discussions. At the end of the lesson 'he just disappeared' and Jill felt 'quite flat'. Other colleagues within the department also commented on the lack of feedback at the end of individual lessons.

Apart from this incident, Jill felt that she tried to teach as she normally would have done, although she admitted that she delayed some work on *The Pied Piper* until the inspection week because she knew it always went well. During another lesson, she recalls noticing that Martin Bunyan talked to two pupils whose books he had scrutinised. After the lesson she asked the pupils what he had been asking:

> What he'd asked was whether they realised the different implications in the red and the green marking in their books. And they had explained that they really did know the difference. The difference between the red and the green marking is that the red marking is confidence marking and the green marking is their National Curriculum level. And he'd been checking that they knew the difference.

Barbara Wynne felt that a lot of her staff had 'played safe' in their teaching and consequently 'some of them were disappointed at the report'. Carol Fisher sought to teach as she normally did, although she suspected that some of her colleagues within the English department 'slipped in some star lessons'.

> We were certainly up front and moving around all the time, which in real life you can't do every lesson. So to a certain extent he did see us at our best. But, of course, you can't produce what you're not producing regularly.

As the week drew to its close, the English department were preparing themselves for the oral report from Martin Bunyan. Jill Walsh 'expected it to be OK', although she was 'slightly wary' because she wondered what the inspector might have noticed that 'needed changing'. However, she was generally quite optimistic because she felt that Martin Bunyan had appeared from the outset 'to be on our side'. Carol Fisher had an 'unofficial' report back from Martin before she received the formal feedback, so she felt very positive before the latter began. However, she was warned by a colleague to 'stay calm, accept it on the chin', because this colleague felt that no report could be that good and there would always be faults identified. In the event, she had no need to worry:

> First of all, he said it had been an honour to be in the department. And I was very touched by this. Well, he came up with all these favourable things and I was terribly touched, after all these years of being thought of as retrograde and old fashioned. But all the time I was waiting for the sting in the tail! And the registered inspector was watching me and smiling. I could see that he was

actually enjoying seeing my pleasure. And that was really quite an unforgettable moment that I've never had before in the profession. To have your department analysed and praised, it was really a rare moment in my life.

Jill Walsh went into Carol's classroom immediately after the oral feedback to find out how it had gone. There she found Carol and the deputy headteacher 'thrilled to bits' at what had been said, particularly the comments that came from the registered inspector that Martin Bunyan wasn't prone to being over-generous. So they were 'all very excited'. And Carol Fisher 'ran to tell as many people as possible'.

After the inspection

At the end of the week, after the inspection team left the premises, the staff held a small celebratory party, but Barbara Wynne felt that everyone was feeling 'brain-dead' at this stage and that her staff were 'very quiet, very subdued' during this party. In some ways she thought the whole week had been 'a bit of an anti-climax because of all that we'd done leading up to it'. This sense of anti-climax was also felt by Jill Walsh:

> You are aware of how much more you would like to have shown them, particularly as the response to us was good. You go on feeling to some extent that you would like to carry on showing them things they didn't see. But then you're not able to, you just have to carry on teaching. It's very, very difficult. It is an anti-climax I think but an anti-climax in that you still carry on. We'd put a lot of work into preparing for that one week and I suppose we were on a high for that week without realising it and suddenly that had finished.

Carol Fisher felt 'justified in standing out for the things that one felt important though others didn't – spelling, punctuation and so on'. This sense of elation stayed with her for some days but the next three weeks of term she 'felt like a zombie', because of the sense of relief and the feeling of exhaustion. She was surprised how openly some of her colleagues in other departments spoke about their problems, 'which didn't happen normally'.

The registered inspector returned two weeks later to read the draft report to the senior management team. Barbara Wynne's first reaction after hearing the report was, 'Is this really Axminster?' and she recalls feeling 'relief, a certain amount of pride and also satisfaction, because it was coming over as a very positive report'. In some ways, however, she was disappointed:

> I had actually hoped that the inspection might have picked up a few more critical points, that would have been a kind of weapon for me to use to move

the staff forward. Because having got a good inspection, a lot of staff's attitude was, 'Well, we don't need to do anything now, do we?' And yet there are lots of things that we still need to do.

She was pleased for the English department and for Carol Fisher in particular because she was aware of how much they had 'moved forward' in recent years, though she felt that there was more work to do in the areas of special needs and drama and was sorry that the English report had not identified these.

Martin Bunyan's report on English at Axminster Modern School, after praising the standards achieved in GCSE examinations, includes comments on speaking and listening, where 'pupils attain high levels of achievement', the range of reading materials which include 'a suitable emphasis on pre-twentieth century texts and... a range of poetry', and pupils' writing, where 'pupils are encouraged to think imaginatively and creatively with a considerable amount of poetry and descriptive work being produced, as well as writing in a variety of styles, including the informative and persuasive'. The report also praises the 'detailed planning' within the English department and the 'variety of approaches' used by teachers.

Jill Walsh was 'thrilled' with this report when it was finally published some weeks later 'because it was so positive'. Carol Fisher was also pleased, because 'it was pretty much as expected', although there was a comment which referred to girls' achievements at GCSE being 'considerably better than boys'.

All departments were asked by headteacher Barbara Wynne after the inspection to create their own development plan, based on the whole-school plan but addressing the issues identified in the inspection report. A departmental development plan was drawn up at an English department meeting, including steps to improve boys' examination results, which identified an intention to 'research new texts for boys', to 'spend more time checking homework notebooks' and to 'insist on better paragraphs' as part of this drive to improve boys' performance.

Jill Walsh pointed out other areas of the department's development plan which she felt were important, particularly more IT development, more drama, and, especially, more collaborative work, so that teachers with particular expertise such as the head of drama and technology staff would team-teach with members of the English department. She felt that the OFSTED inspection process had led the department to share their ideas and resources more than had occurred before:

> We're much more aware now of the schemes that we've written and making them available, not just keeping the scheme but putting it into a bank. And also we are aware that, when we do a text that already has a scheme, we can

add to it various things that we're discovering. For example, there's much more for special needs now, adapting texts that we have and developing and adapting activities to suit the special needs children.

She felt that members of the department were working more closely together since the inspection:

Because of having the need to present everything in black and white for OFSTED, now it's there for the whole department to see, it's gelling much more.

Final perceptions

Jill Walsh – second in English department
I think it's made us more aware. We work as individuals and maybe that's wrong, but it's so easy, especially when you've been in the profession for a number of years, to know what you want to do and to get on with it and perhaps not to be flexible and adaptable and sharing enough. And, speaking personally, I've been made much more aware of how we do need to share and how we each can benefit from other people's ideas. And it was something like OFSTED which perhaps made this much more obvious. It was also a confidence boost in that it confirmed that what we were doing was alright. It was stressful, although I don't think we realised how much until afterwards.

Carol Fisher – head of English
Obviously, I'm in favour of it, because it was successful from our point of view. And I suppose that inspecting good schools like ours gives the inspectors ammunition to pull up the 5 per cent of poor schools. It's made me slightly more arrogant than I was before! But I do feel validated. And that is very important.

Barbara Wynne – headteacher
I have mixed views really. It hasn't told us anything we didn't already know but it has brought everything together. We have had an external audit of the school which I think will be useful as a starting point for the next four years. It's certainly useful for some of the weaker curriculum areas, because we now have a typed Action Plan of what they've got to do and how they're going to do it. I think it's done the school some good because it has confirmed the school in the locality as an OK school. We're on a high in the area at the moment and people are saying good things about us. The OFSTED report was the most positive of those that

have been produced so far on any of the town's schools. I think it's a very expensive system. I'm sure it could be done more cost-effectively. I wouldn't say it's a waste of time but, in terms of staff stress and staff work, I'm not sure that all the work that went into it has improved the quality of the teaching of the children. If anything, I'd say this term the quality has deteriorated, because staff are absolutely exhausted. When I've talked to some other heads, about six weeks after an inspection, there seems to be an increase in staff absences. The person who does the cover calls it post-inspection syndrome.

CHAPTER 8

Conclusion

The OFSTED enterprise was clearly going to be a considerable one. The creation of a system, which administered tenders and contracts for inspection, which trained and registered large numbers of inspectors, and which monitored the operation of the inspections, was bound to be a mammoth undertaking and one which would certainly take time to establish and which would require regular adjustment. The haste with which central government ushered in the new system was very much in line with its record of legislating in the education sector since 1988. Given such a background and given the inevitable problems that arise when change is legislated for and then enacted so rapidly, many would judge that the OFSTED system was remarkably successful in its first year of operation, certainly in terms of successfully delivering all of the secondary school inspections that it was committed to.

OFSTED's own quality assurance unit, staffed by remaining members of Her Majesty's Inspectorate, has stated publicly that, on the basis of its monitoring of inspections during the inspection weeks and of visiting schools in the weeks immediately after they had been inspected, the vast majority of inspections had been carried out satisfactorily. Schools were generally happy with the way in which inspectors had conducted the inspections, although concerns were expressed about two particular issues – the amount of documentation required and the lack of feedback to individual teachers at the end of lessons.

In the sixth issue of *Update*, the newsletter through which the administrators of OFSTED communicate with inspectors, there is a brief report on maintaining and improving the quality of the inspection system. Revealingly, the authors of the introductory section, Peter Matthews, head of quality assurance and development, and Ian Shelton, head of monitoring, state:

> At the heart of all this activity is a concern for quality. This goes far beyond compliance with regulations, standards and guidance; it is also about professionalism, people and – at its heart – common sense.

It has been our purpose in this book to listen to the people caught up in this new activity, to examine not only their professional reactions to inspection but also their human reactions, and to seek to learn from the experiences of those who have undergone the inspection process in the first year of the newly created OFSTED system. By focusing on the particular experience of English teaching, we hoped to shed some light on the process as perceived by some of those engaged in the task of helping young people to develop their abilities as language users and meaning makers. It seemed to us likely that the articulations of these teachers and inspectors might provide powerful insights whose echoes might be heard in other areas of the curriculum.

In seeking to draw conclusions from the case studies detailed in previous chapters, we are making the assumption that the OFSTED system will continue into the foreseeable future – an assumption which we understand is reasonable, since all major political parties appear committed to the system in principle, notwithstanding the current difficulties in delivering the programme of inspections of primary and special schools.

It seems to us, therefore, that there are important lessons for all the stakeholders – teachers, heads of departments, headteachers, inspectors and OFSTED personnel – to learn from the experiences described in our case studies of six very different schools. Using the pattern of the case studies, and drawing on evidence therein, our findings are presented in the shape of before the inspection, during the inspection and after the inspection.

Before the inspection

Many schools, if not the great majority, are already checking their practices against the *Handbook for the Inspection of Schools*, in the knowledge that sooner or later they will be inspected. In using the *Handbook* thus, many have found it to be a valuable tool for ensuring that their policies and practices are up to date and in order. However, in a sense what these schools are engaged in at this stage is a 'phoney war'. The process of inspection actually begins when a school is first notified by OFSTED that it is due for inspection in a particular term. Such precise knowledge inevitably sharpens practice, as we have seen in most of the case studies in this book, but it also causes considerable anxieties and fuller consideration needs to be given to the nature of these anxieties and to whether there are ways in which some if not all might be eliminated.

Alice Walker of Newton Middle School described her anxiety as being 'the fear of the unknown' and she also expressed concern that it might be 'very much a policing thing'. Helen Roberts of St Augustine's High School described her suspicion of 'people [who] would be watching us who knew nothing about teaching'. Kirsty Wigton of Queen Mary's Grammar School for Girls believed the inspections could be 'more variable in experience from team to team'. These concerns, which are almost certainly echoed throughout schools nationwide, are more to do with the perceived political agenda behind the inspection system than with the inspection process itself. They are not helped by the incautious comments quoted in the *Daily Mail* of Her Majesty's Chief Inspector, Chris Woodhead, on taking up his post in September 1994 about inspections helping to get rid of poor teachers.

It surely would not be impossible for OFSTED to demonstrate more publicly and more powerfully what it sees as the purpose of inspection. The *Framework for Inspection* is perfectly clear. In its opening sentence, it states:

> The purpose of inspection is to identify strengths and weaknesses in schools so that they may improve the quality of education offered and raise the standards achieved by their pupils.

Unfortunately, at present, as we have seen throughout this book, the notion that inspection can lead to improvement is not widely shared. What possible reasons can we suggest for this?

First of all, many teachers see the creation of the OFSTED system as another piece of government legislation designed to cow them into submission and make them deliverers of centrally determined and centrally controlled schooling. The government's track record in legislating for educational change is not good, with constant amendments and backtracking being the norm rather than the exception. If OFSTED is to escape from this pattern – and there are reasons to believe that in its first year of operation it has gone some way to do so – then it needs to distance itself more obviously from the Department for Education. It would help if all political parties would pledge themselves to its long-term continuation, even though any newly elected government might seek adjustments to its operational patterns.

Secondly, we suspect that large numbers of inspectors share teachers' perceptions – Jack Eliot was concerned about 'political notions of accountability', Matthew Dickens was concerned because of losing the 'developmental thrust' of LEA inspections and Janet Woolf from different experience knew how teachers 'hate and fear observation'. Many strive to bring a humane face to their work, as we have seen notably in Queen Mary's Grammar School where English inspector Michael Peacock was seen by the English teachers as 'willing to look for good things' and 'always very positive about the girls', in St Augustine's where English inspector Jack Eliot was seen as presenting himself 'in a very quiet, unassuming, unaggressive way immediately', and in Bingley Community School where English inspector Colin Forster was seen as 'extremely friendly, not aggressive in any way'. As former HMI Trevor Dickinson shows in his opening chapter, such concerns and such humane faces are not new. Under the previous regime of HMI inspections, similar anxieties and similar ways of handling such anxieties were apparent.

Inspectors' attitudes and perceptions are equally as important as those of the teachers whose work they are examining. If there is a genuine wish to create a long-term inspection system to replace HMI, then there is a need at some point to address the issue of how to create and maintain the 'interpretive community'[1] which HMI believed itself to be. In the field of English teaching, such an 'interpretive community' exists in the National Association for the Teaching of English, whose members include many English inspectors, and in the National Association of Advisers in English (NAAE), which originally was composed of LEA English advisers and inspectors but has recently broadened its membership to include those working independently. Both associations are currently considering their links with OFSTED but, as with the previous HMI system, such links are likely at present to remain informal. Again, it would seem sensible that, if OFSTED is to have a long life-span, it needs to seek ways of formalising those links with subject associations in order to strengthen that 'interpretive community', although it is important to bear in mind Trevor Dickinson's warning that 'Objective judgement is a myth.'

It needs to be said that the sort of changes outlined above would represent a considerable cultural move. However able individual HMIs were under the old system – and many people in this book speak highly of their contacts with HMI – their practice was essentially secretive. In an era of open government, where the *Handbook for the Inspection of Schools* is a publicly available document, such secretiveness needs to be dispelled. It is unfortunate that the remaining HMIs are the guardians of the new system, since they inevitably draw on their former practice to

---

1 We are grateful to Graham Frater, former staff HMI for English, for this useful term taken from the work of Stanley Fish on literary theory.

guide their thinking. It was HMI who were responsible for developing and initially leading the training of inspectors, which resulted in Matthew Dickens feeling 'physically sick, emotionally and professionally very discomfited' and in Colin Forster's sense of 'being watched all the time'. If a genuine 'interpretive community' in English teaching is to develop, then NATE, NAAE and English HMI within OFSTED need to commence an open dialogue.

Greater openness, then, about OFSTED's real purpose and about the values in English teaching, as opposed to the mechanics of delivering National Curriculum English, would, we believe, be welcome improvements to the present pattern and would reduce much of the anxiety felt by English teachers when they contemplate the forthcoming inspection of their practice.

As part of this greater openness, it is certainly true that those English teachers interviewed in order to gain the evidence for this book felt more comfortable and confident when they had some prior knowledge of their English inspector, even when such knowledge was based on hearsay. Paul Lawrence of Bingley Community School was 'reassured by hearing from an English advisory teacher in the city and from one of my tutors at the university that Colin Forster was alright', Helen Roberts of St Augustine's High School was able to tell her departmental colleagues that Jack Eliot 'came recommended' because she 'knew personally people who thought that [he] was a good chap'. Don Meadows of Sheriff High School, a member of NATE, was pleased to learn that the registered inspector 'was someone who had been involved in that organisation'. On the other hand, Kirsty Wigton of Queen Mary's Grammar School had no prior knowledge of Michael Peacock, who inspected English in her school, and only felt confident at the end of the inspection week to ask him 'where he was from and what was his background and what was his past'. It is clearly important for English teachers, particularly heads of departments, to learn as early as possible of the background of their inspectors. Equally clearly, the knowledge that English inspectors are part of the 'interpretive community' described above, either through the personal recommendation of a respected colleague elsewhere within the education system or as a member of one of the two major associations concerned with English, influences the view that English teachers take. This must have an inevitable impact on the confidence with which they approach the inspection.

Two other issues concerning pre-inspection matters emerge from the case studies. The first is related to the preparation of documentation for the OFSTED inspectors and the second is related to the formal pre-inspection scrutinies offered to schools by a range of agencies, often, but not exclusively, from the LEA in which the school is situated.

OFSTED inspectors are required to complete a thorough pre-inspection schedule of general issues, which involves them in scrutinising the documentation provided by the school and forming hypotheses from such scrutiny in order to determine issues they might wish to explore during the period of the inspection. It is essential for such documentation to be made available to inspectors. Those who are inspecting subjects are sometimes required by their registered inspector to complete a similar pre-inspection commentary but this practice, which would overcome the concern that has been expressed in some quarters about under-preparation by inspectors, is not widespread.

Many headteachers use the opportunity of their OFSTED inspection to require their subject departments to up-date their documentation, sometimes to a common format and often in a common style of presentation. Joyce Sedgley of Queen Mary's Grammar School echoed the views of many of her fellow head teachers when she stated that 'the impression that is made on the inspection team starts as soon as they receive the schemes of work'. For some English departments, this is an onerous task, as Paul Lawrence of Bingley Community School discovered when 'spending numerous hours at the computer contributing to the handbook', while for others it can be a way of bringing about a greater sharing of ideas, as pointed out by Jill Walsh of Axminster Secondary School:

> We do have now a much more methodical means of tying together all these different schemes and all the schemes are now more readily available.

On the other hand, an English department that is already working in common and agreed ways, that has a clear and shared ethos, and whose documentation is already in a good state need have no worries, as Don Meadows of Sheriff High School found. All teachers need to take note of the warning from Mavis Bentley of St Augustine's High School – 'In spite of all the documentation... what they are really looking at is the quality of teaching and learning.'

A variety of pre-inspection preparations was undertaken by the schools in our case studies – teachers observing each other teaching using the OFSTED Lesson Observation Pro-forma at Newton Middle School, a scrutiny of departmental documentation by subject specialist LEA advisers at St Augustine's High School, a day's mini-inspection of the department by subject specialist LEA advisers at Queen Mary's Grammar School and at Axminster Secondary School, attendance at conferences by teachers from Newton Middle School and from Bingley Community School. The reactions of the teachers concerned to these pre-inspection scrutinies were mixed. Both Kirsty Wigton and Audrey Wright of Queen Mary's Grammar School found the mini-inspection visit helpful because it 'reassured us that inspectors were human beings and the kind of people we had been working with all the time'. Carol Fisher of Axminster Modern School also found the visit by her LEA's English inspector valuable, admitting to being 'most impressed' because 'she suggested that we started renewing the schemes of work'. On the other hand, the mini-inspection experienced by Bingley Community School which did not involve an English specialist, was felt to be 'of no value whatsoever personally or to the department' by the English staff.

The issue of classroom observation is an interesting one, because it would appear from these case studies that teachers who have experienced formal classroom observation as part of appraisal cope more easily with such as part of an inspection. On the other hand, the decision by Francis Johnston, headteacher of Newton Middle School, to issue his staff with copies of the OFSTED Lesson Observation Pro-forma, in order for them to complete these during observation of each other's lessons, was almost certainly responsible for head of English Alice Walker's anxiety about the lesson she describes when three children read their short stories to the rest of the class:

> But then I thought if I was actually observing this lesson, would there have been enough variety? Would there have been enough pace?

It certainly was responsible for her colleague's attempt 'to fit her lesson to the pro-forma'.

Throughout the case studies, one of the most consistent features is how the attitude of the headteacher towards the inspection process is crucial. All the headteachers were sceptical about the value of the OFSTED system; all were just as naturally concerned that the findings of their school's inspection were accurate and positive. Consequently, in every case headteachers sought to manage the inspection in ways that they felt would be most beneficial to their schools. In general it would appear that, where a headteacher determined that the inspection should be viewed in a positive light and seen as a contribution to the school's development, it inevitably was so. This was certainly the case at St Augustine's High School and at Sheriff High School. Both Bill Wright of Bingley Community School and Barbara Wynne of Axminster Secondary School found the inspection to be a validation of the work of their schools rather more than as a contribution to development, while Joyce Sedgley, though accepting the validation possibilities particularly at departmental level, felt that the whole inspection process had been 'an interruption to the serious work that has to be done in the school'. Francis Johnston's attitude to the inspection was perhaps more concerned with the tension between Newton Middle School, with its newly acquired grant-maintained status, and its former LEA, whose inspectorate won the OFSTED contract to inspect the school, than in the event it needed to be.

During the inspection

For all the English teachers and English inspectors in this book, the inspection proper begins on the first morning when they are in school together. All the documents have been written and read, all the lessons have been prepared, all the preliminaries have been completed. It is perhaps not surprising that the first day of an OFSTED inspection, after all the preparation that has taken place – 'the vacuuming of the carpets' referred to by Matthew Dickens – should induce the tensions and anxieties that are reported in our case studies. Helen Roberts's inability to eat her breakfast (St Augustine's High), Brenda Royce's apprehensiveness (Newton Middle), Audrey Wright's panic at not being able to use the photocopier (Queen Mary's Grammar) and Paul Lawrence's numbness during staff briefing (Bingley Community) seem typical responses. It is also important to point out how younger and less experienced members of English departments feel that they might be responsible for the 'failure' of the department – Audrey Wright, again, worrying about 'letting the side down', Fiona Ingles's concern about 'letting the department down' (St Augustine's High).

Although there is no formal requirement for them to do so, all but one of the English inspectors in this book arranged an early meeting with the heads of English. Such meetings, which are usually for the English inspector to seek further information about the work of the department or clarification of some of the documentation, serve as the first stage in the human interaction which has to apply in an OFSTED inspection week. Impressions gained by Heads of English at this stage tend to last throughout the week. Sensitive inspectors who demonstrate a willingness to listen, who are 'unassuming and unaggressive', who give praise, who avoid 'OFSTED-speak' as much as possible, as all of the English inspectors in these case studies did, are more likely to be perceived as fellow professionals whose views and perceptions are worth heeding.

Generally speaking, it would appear that the earlier such a formal contact is made, the better. Michael Peacock was able to meet Kirsty Wigton before the school day began at Queen Mary's Grammar, Martin Bunyan met Jill Walsh at Axminster Modern during the second period of the day, Jack Eliot at St Augustine's and Colin Forster at Bingley

Community met their respective heads of English early in the first day. Janet Woolf's first meeting with Don Meadows of Sheriff High, on the other hand, came during a lunchtime computer club, which he found 'a bit awkward'. The most problematic meeting was that between Matthew Dickens and Alice Walker at Newton Middle, which couldn't be timetabled during the school day because Alice had no non-contact time available. Consequently, Matthew had already spent two days observing English lessons before he formally spoke to Alice and the meeting also coincided with a day when she was on duty. The misunderstanding that arose during that meeting and which affected Alice's perceptions of the inspection for the rest of the week, until she received her feedback, was probably attributable to the unfortunate timing of this meeting.

There were no serious problems reported by teachers from the lesson observations in our case studies. Once the inspection was under way and English departments had realised that their English inspectors had a sound and thoroughly professional understanding of English teaching, they generally relaxed. In many cases, the heightened awareness brought about by the inspection and the 'adrenalin' referred to by several teachers resulted in some outstanding lessons. It also appears that, despite the constraints of time and no doubt the warnings to staff by registered inspectors, all of the English inspectors found some time to comment briefly to teachers at the end of lessons. Where they were unable to do so, as in the case of Martin Bunyan who 'just disappeared' at the end of one lesson taught by Jill Walsh at Axminster Modern leaving her feeling 'quite flat', teachers found the experience less satisfactory. Clearly, from the evidence in this book, it is not impossible for English inspectors to make brief comments at the end of lessons which refer to the quality of learning in the classroom and which can therefore be received as supportive and helpful.

It is also worth remembering the comments of Paul Lawrence of Bingley Community School, a young teacher who is aware that he is still learning his craft and is consequently keen for constructive criticism:

> I can't see why professionals can't sit down and talk about lessons and open the gateway to professional development. To have someone of Colin Forster's experience come in and not be able to comment to me on what he saw is just loopy.

Inevitably an inspection can only glimpse the work of an English department by scrutinising it during one week. In preparing for that week, English departments have to take a view of how 'normal' their teaching will be. There is no clear evidence from our case studies of any department or of any teacher seeking to teach lessons in ways never tried beforehand. As Carol Fisher of Axminster Modern pointed out, 'You can't produce what you're not producing regularly.'

However, all the English departments wanted to be seen at their best and a variety of approaches is noticeable. Several teachers admitted to saving a particular set of lessons which they knew worked well until the inspection week and the English department at St Augustine's High included more drama and oral work than they would normally do within one week. Staff at Queen Mary's Grammar, acting on advice from the LEA English inspector who had visited them previously, drew Michael Peacock's attention to folders of IT work to demonstrate the extent of their use of IT.

Apparently minor incidents in the interaction between English inspectors and English teachers during the inspection week can be taken out of all proportion by the heads of English, because of the tensions of the week and because the inspector is, as Don Meadows of Sheriff High pointed out, 'for that week an important person'. In his case the incident was over a request by Janet Woolf for lesson notes from a non-specialist member of the English department, which that teacher was unable to give. Despite Janet Woolf's subsequent apology, Don Meadows reported 'a bit of a hurt atmosphere' for the rest of that day and also his admittedly irrational concern that he might get his 'come-uppance when this report was written', because he had told his headteacher about the incident. The misunderstanding already referred to between Matthew Dickens and Alice Walker at Newton Middle also seriously affected her perceptions of the English feedback. She reported that she thought she had 'blown it' and admitted that she had 'actually picked up totally the wrong messages'.

Of more serious concern is the impact of the oral report by the English inspector to the head of English, usually delivered near to the end of the time in school. The quite correct insistence to inspectors during their training that there should be nothing in the final written report that has not already been said to the teachers concerned during the inspection has led to the common practice whereby a member of the school's senior management attends each subject debriefing in order to take detailed notes and to support departmental heads. Inspectors are being encouraged to read their interim report on the teaching of the subject inspected and they normally are doing this from the Record of Evidence which they are required to complete.

The formality of this feedback process, often in a deputy headteacher's office and sometimes with the registered inspector present as well, is certainly preventing much in the way of dialogue between the two main players – the head of English and the English inspector – from taking place. In all cases, English inspectors were looking to praise the positive aspects of practice that they had witnessed, for example Michael Peacock at Queen Mary's Grammar 'wanted to pay an objective tribute to the quality of the department'. Some English inspectors also wanted to point up ways forward, for example Colin Forster at Bingley Community School felt he could 'identify many good features in the department' and show 'areas for development'.

Apart from Kirsty Wigton of Queen Mary's Grammar School, who was disappointed in her report back because she 'heard the "satisfactories"' rather than all the much more positive comments which she subsequently found in the written report, the heads of English in our case studies were happy with the feedback that they received. However, the limitations of vocabulary which OFSTED has forced on to inspectors is clearly very problematic and the change of wording from 'satisfactory' to 'sound' in the revision to the *Framework* for autumn 1994 is unlikely to alter this. It is also important for English teachers to note the comment of Helen Roberts from St Augustine's High School on receiving the written report that 'the warmth had gone from it'.

Matthew Dickens raised the important issue of why the Subject Record of Evidence forms have to be 'secret documents'. It is our belief, having looked at large numbers of these, that they could quite validly be given to schools as internal documents for their own use after an inspection. This would reduce the need for the extensive note-taking by members of senior management at oral feedbacks and be a useful developmental tool for the department and the school.

After the inspection

Without exception, every English teacher interviewed for this book spoke of the feelings of exhaustion and relief they experienced when the actual inspection was over. This was true even for those who confessed to having been given a boost by the reported findings. It is also not unusual to find that many English departments experience a dip in their performance over the following few weeks.

Schools are required by law to produce an Action Plan after an OFSTED inspection, which explains how the school will be dealing with the key issues identified in the report. Some schools, for instance Sheriff High, Axminster and St Augustine's, have used this as an opportunity to create a new School Development Plan. In the case of St Augustine's High School, this was done by requiring each subject department to outline plans for addressing issues identified in the oral feedback from their inspector and recorded by a member of the senior management. A similar pattern was observed at Axminster Secondary School. In the case of Sheriff High, it was done by seeking to involve all departments in giving their response to each of the key issues identified in the inspection report. In other schools, Action Plans have been created largely at senior management level. It is too early to comment on the effectiveness or usefulness of these Action Plans.

One of the major concerns, expressed by both teachers and inspectors, is with the lack of contact between the department and the English inspector after the event. In many ways this is inevitable, given the nature of the contracting system by which OFSTED awards contracts, which means that inspection teams may be drawn from different parts of the country making subsequent contact difficult. However, there is a need for some kind of networking system to develop, if there is to be maximum value in OFSTED inspections as ways of improving practice. The approach adopted at St Augustine's High School, where the LEA's English inspector is to spend time with the English department helping them to address issues identified by Jack Eliot is praiseworthy but easier sharing of information between English inspectors and those who may subsequently be called in to give professional help needs to be developed.

It is perhaps surprising that public reaction to individual OFSTED inspections of schools has been apparently muted, since it was clearly a government intention that the publication of inspection reports would be of value to parents and potential parents. Again it is too early to pass judgement on the latter intention, although comments at Axminster and at Newton Middle suggest that successful reports may influence parental choice.

It is also too soon to attempt any judgements about the effectiveness of the OFSTED inspection of English in shaping practice in the teaching and learning of English. Apart from one or two teachers who referred to a perceived need to foreground their work with grammar and spelling, the English departments in the case studies within this book seemed confident in their own practice and confident that they could demonstrate that practice, sometimes at its best, during the inspection week. Nowhere was there a sense that classroom practice had to change to meet the commonly perceived government agenda relating to Standard English, the literary heritage, 'back to basics' in formal language teaching and didactic teaching. Indeed, as Helen Roberts of St Augustine's High School pointed out, 'The department afterwards felt very secure that the paths that were being trod were definitely OK.'

Final perceptions

It is our belief that the OFSTED inspection process can be a powerful weapon for change, if it is harnessed. For this to happen, it needs to be genuinely freed from government interference and to be allowed to operate – indeed encouraged, if not instructed, to operate – in ways which are designed to improve schools, rather than simply to provide information for the central OFSTED database to enable Her Majesty's Chief Inspector to report on the state of education. Clearly this latter is an important element of the work of a national inspection system but at present it appears to be driving the system rather than being one side of a two-way system, perhaps because the tenor of the inspection process was modelled on the practice of HMI. Indeed, the *Handbook for the Inspection of Schools* was compiled by HMI and the training and assessment of would-be inspectors was initially carried out by HMI, as has already been pointed out.

As far as English is concerned, the experiences of those who have contributed to this book suggest that teachers with confidence in their approaches and policies need have nothing to worry about from an OFSTED inspection. Despite all the wrangles over the content of National Curriculum English in recent years, and perhaps at times because of those wrangles, English departments in secondary schools in general appear to have a strong set of principles for how they will work with their pupils.

Most English departments have had some involvement with the major English-related projects of the 1980s – the National Writing Project, the National Oracy Project and the Language in the National Curriculum (LINC) Project and the experience derived from such involvement has clearly had a major impact on thinking and practice. Almost all English departments also moved quite rapidly to the adoption of the 100 per cent coursework option as the fairest and most appropriate way of assessing their pupils' English achievements at GCSE. The incredible unanimity of support illustrated by the 'Save English Coursework' campaign demonstrates how powerfully this adoption of the 100 per cent coursework option has affected English teachers' thinking and understanding of their subject. This is exemplified in the comments arising from the OFSTED inspection made by Doug Collins, acting head of English at Bingley Community School: 'You get a clearer picture of your own values, your own expectations of pupils, your own approaches to the subject.'

We must also not underestimate the influence of NATE in all of this. Through its regular newsletters and journals, through its enhanced publications list, which currently includes excellent classroom materials produced by the English and Media Centre in London, and through its ability to make its voice heard in the national media, NATE has had a major impact on the way that English teachers perceive themselves and are perceived. The growth in NATE membership throughout the 1980s is an indication of how more and more English teachers and departments were looking for the intellectual, pedagogical and political support that NATE has been able to provide. NATE's sister association, the NAAE, has had a similar impact on its members, many of whom are currently engaged as OFSTED English inspectors.

Our anxiety, then, is not so much about how English departments cope with OFSTED but with how OFSTED can become a developmental agent. There are indications in our case studies of how this might happen and is probably already happening, as Jack Eliot, English inspector at St Augustine's High School, pointed out:

> There are opportunities to bring about improvement in a much more general way. And part of that is to be able to recognise strengths and praise those strengths rather than simply identifying weaknesses.

At the end of the day, we will need to account for the success or failure of any new educational initiative, not in terms of the reams of paper that it produced but in terms of the standards of achievement reached by the pupils in our schools.